The Invisible Voice

GEORGE KONRÁD

The Invisible Voice

Meditations on Jewish Themes

Translated from the Hungarian by Peter Reich

A Harvest Original
A Helen and Kurt Wolff Book
Harcourt, Inc.

SAN DIEGO   NEW YORK   LONDON

Requests for permission to make copies
of any part of the work should be mailed to:
Permissions Department, Harcourt, Inc.,
6277 Sea Harbor Drive, Orlando, Florida 32887-6777.

Library of Congress Cataloging-in-Publication Data
Konrád, György.
The invisible voice: meditations on Jewish themes/George Konrád;
translated from the Hungarian by Peter Reich.
p.   cm.
"A Harvest original."
"A Helen and Kurt Wolff book."
ISBN 0-15-601294-4
1. Jews—Hungary—Miscellanea. 2. Holocaust, Jewish (1939–1945)
3. Judaism—20th century. 4. Jews—Hungary—Identity.
5. Hungary—Ethnic relations.   I. Title.
DS135.H9 K63   2000
943.9′004924—dc21   99-047036

Text set in Janson
Designed by Camilla Filancia
Printed in the United States of America
First Edition
A C E D B

Table of Contents

The Invisible Voice

Citizen or Subject

1. The ruling ideals of the twentieth century were without exception murderous ideals, though none set out to murder. Reason enough for communities and civilizations proud of their ideals to be disconcerted, to look inward and try to discover what went wrong at home, first of all. In our century how many mass graves originated from the mixed metaphors of lettered men!

The events of history generally signify the violent death of many people. The right murdered, and the left murdered. They murdered nearby, and they murdered far away. All nationalities murdered, some with extraordinary diligence. The wealthy murdered, and the poor murdered; the elderly murdered, and the young murdered. Women and children murdered relatively little.

No form of the first person plural is harmless. Even the community of writers can reflect on a rather ugly past; able wielders of the pen justified and gilded all manner of infamy, or at least supported it with their silence.

2. What is one person capable of doing for another? How trustworthy are we? When do you betray another? I am not gullible. I do not believe people are good by nature. I know the battle, the contest of passions is eternal; only the combatants change.

The one wants to overcome the other, either from fear or from envy. Whether one is rich or poor makes no difference. Those who have are just as keen to spend their fury as those who have not.

Evil is an independent force, not just misunderstanding and not just the absence of good. Knowing that the life of another person is frail only makes some more inclined to take it.

And the angel of bad faith gives murder a legal title. It says: the life of a particular person is not sacred. It makes abstract concepts sacred and acquits of guilt, so that a perplexed person without a guide can fall under the spell of crime.

3. How was it possible to kill four and a half million of us, four and a half million Jews? Why didn't the elderly and even children defend themselves, with knives at least? We should have killed that small group of people capable of accelerating nationalist socialist momentum into the paroxysm of mass murder. Few of us were as brave as the residents of the Warsaw ghetto.

Those who do not resist are merely objects. I approve the ethic of resistance, spiritual-intellectual resistance if the aggressors do not intend murder, armed resistance if they do.

The Jewish people bear some of the responsibility for becoming victims in such horrifying proportions. Our fathers were negligent; they weakened themselves with learned ideas. They came to have a naive spiritual dependence on the local authorities. Under the guise of patriotic loyalty, the fascist states expected Jews to give disciplined approval to their own destruction. To line up on the gangplank above the frozen Danube. After taking a bullet in the back of the head, Jews should tumble into the hole in the ice one after the other, into the cavity axed into the ice sheet. Mothers should quiet their weeping children. By carrying out orders in a disciplined manner in this difficult hour, our fellow countrymen of the Israelite faith can prove they are loyal subjects of our state.

4. Forty years later, I find that old Jewish men still cannot recover from the murder of their young wives and small children. They still do not understand why they should forget them. There are scars that cannot heal.

I want to believe that violent death does not destroy the meaning of the murdered person's life. I want to believe that our presence and exertions here were not in vain.

Nevertheless, I maintain that we erred gravely. The duty of the parent is to protect the life of the child. Even if the parent is killed for it. Those who obey the guard or the hangman commit the sin of cowardice.

5. If a person wants to get hold of an ideology easily, quickly, the most expedient way is to hate. Those who do not dare to declare everyone their enemy will find a smaller group, one hated with less risk. Hating a minority group is the most convenient option.

How can competitors be slandered? Among many methods, one is to say they are not patriotic enough. The word *patriotic* may be replaced by another, but this charge has proved quite effective in most countries. If the wheel begins to turn and patriotism begins to rumble, great patriots are replaced by even greater patriots at decreasing intervals.

The fusion of national hatred and majority hatred eases the path of those with a great capacity to hate, and helps them turn their hatred always in the appropriate direction. Being a passionate member of the majority is generally advantageous, a good career move. Explosive and extravagant hostility is most often an attribute of armed men who are sure the enemy cannot fight back.

To organize pogroms against the hated minority in the name of the hating majority is sweet, mad gratification. Pitching that infant against the wall, raping that virgin, and dragging that old man through the muck by his beard are deeds that can remain unpunished only in the carnival of the pogrom; only then can they be given moral approbation by the majority. The pogrom is a transnational holiday. Not a year passes on earth without one, but it can be said that Jews have historical experience of the similarity between pogroms and brushfires.

6. We cannot be too aggressive in the first person singular; we will be ostracized or branded criminals. If we express our aggression in the first person plural, however, we may even get a statue dedicated to us.

The interior of communal consciousness can be characterized by a certain greasy, sweaty desire to become part of a crowd. Moist-eyed people wanting to exchange confidences. It is their habit to embrace as well, like drunks—which doesn't stop them from taking mortal offense a minute later. Sooner or later, in the most divergent of communities, I smelled the raw, intimate foot odor of a military tent, heavy-handed cheer, an imbecilic self-confidence: We are the special ones.

If I am in a room with someone suffering from some consciousness of minority, I anticipate the moment when sentimental brutality will emerge.

7. It would not be precise to assert that nations on the road to embourgoisement—Germans in the vanguard—liked themselves too much, and killed Jews in an excess of self-love. No, the problem was that they did not believe their own boasting. They would have got along better with us had they got along better with themselves.

But only the Germans had the capability to carry out the paranoid idea of annihilating the Jews with such perfect circumspection. No other people could have got so far in annihilating us, the only one as methodical as they. Other peoples would have grown lax; halfway or a third of the way through, they would have grown bored with exterminating Jews.

All nations are on the road to humanity, but before they get there, every one gets caught up in some sort of anguished delusion of grandeur. At those times, they lose their reason and are capable of anything.

In their paroxysm of nationalism, the Germans avenged on us their having to step beyond German-only philistinism, for we were their predecessors on the way to Europe and to becoming citizens of the world.

8. Speaking with German friends in West Berlin, I am less confused about being Hungarian and Jewish than I am in Budapest. Neither Hungarian nor Jewish is German; they are both something else. Without assimilation, without dissimulation, I try to live in harmony with my environment. I am biased in favor of Hungarians and Jews, I feel solidarity with both. I am more fond of the community of fifteen million Hungarians and the community of fifteen million Jews than of other nations.

We do not search for the truth because we are rewarded for finding it. And we do not consider a community our own because it rewards us. We consider it our own because we choose it. And we choose it by working on its behalf—in the manner in which we see fit.

9. Which value system holds the human personality to be an end in itself, and holds its complex particularity to be of higher value than its group characteristics? I don't believe that being similar is more productive than being different.

Anti-Semitism has made Jews smarter. Withholding material values from people makes them turn toward spiritual-intellectual values. This disciplined transcendence trains the mind.

One may esteem people for the variety of attributes they possess. One may promote relationships of harmonic coexistence. We may take account of the complexity of the human phenomenon. It is better to speak two languages than just one. While traveling sometimes, our spiritual reserve relaxes its grip, and in the dizziness of unanticipated sympathies we may actually find attractive the quality of being different.

In the company of composed, tactful, fair, trustworthy, and ironic people, I think of civilization with respect.

10. Unofficial impulses in Eastern European countries are tinted nationalist rather than liberal. If the practice of liberalism is not present, why should its spirit be? After withdrawing from the state-socialist ego, many are drawn to an ego that encourages us to view all issues from the standpoint of nation. Communal morale checks for the other person's group membership rather than for his personality. The exclusionary delimitation of national consciousness is structured much like that of class consciousness. A considerable portion of the literature in our century has been awash in national and class arrogance.

Since childhood, I have always had reservations about being present in a community. I shy away from people who cannot imagine better company than their own.

We are both rational and aggressive; generally our intelligence serves our aggressiveness. Every ideology of community is the system of argumentation for a type of group aggression.

Nationalism's demand—Decide what you are, and be nothing else—is based on abstract speculation. It is an impossible wish, it denies the multifaceted nature of human reality. Human reality is plural; why would we want it to be monolithic?

The nationalist wish is for me to be the mirror of the nation-state. I am not. In no community have I been the man of the majority, disturbed by a minority that is different, urging the difference be smoothed away. I find this boorish majority mentality the classic form of societal stupidity.

I have found that little men feel bigger in consequence of their country's statistical bigness. I have spoken with citizens of nations with large populations; they were filled with the self-satisfaction of being many.

I find Icelanders the most likable of the peoples I have met thus far. I believe there are only two hundred thousand of them. They have been literate for eight hundred years, and they live in democracy.

11. Without democracy, there is discrimination, and as a reaction to negative discrimination, the consciousness of being chosen appears among those discriminated against.

In a democracy, the Jewish consciousness of being chosen is a laughable enough tick alongside the many hundred other kinds of aristocratic minority pride. I find comical the Jew proud of the Torah, Talmud, and Cabala though he doesn't know them. The same goes for the Frenchman who feels exceptional among Europeans on account of Racine and Baudelaire, whom he hasn't read.

In New York, Jewish differentness is perceived with humor, like Italian or Chinese differentness. If they smile or laugh at us, they won't kill us.

12. I've spent half a century in Hungary; if I were to weigh the proportion of Hungarian to Jewish culture in myself, the Hungarian part would be greater. Perhaps a third type is born of the two, a metaphor.

I'm inclined to let myself be characterized by my thinking rather than by an attribute of birth. Why should I be proud of my personal data? Everyone has personal data; it is no accomplishment.

From the nationalist viewpoint, my being Hungarian is dubious, though even my great-great-grandfather was born in a certain village in Bihar. My being Jewish, however, has never been called into question.

The intellectual force of Diaspora Jews originated from their complex mix of attributes. They lived at the intersections of cultures; they had sharper insight into the relativity of human affairs.

As a Jew of the Diaspora, I remain a question until my death, one I will never be able to answer satisfactorily. I will live with my paradoxes. Even though life's most important dilemmas cannot be resolved, one can live with them.

In every city—mine too—I find a few people who are happy to be my friends. Most likely, there are some who think of me with antipathy, as a Jew; those people do not call on me. I'm more interested in whom I like than in who likes me.

Since World War II, anti-Semitism has not been an official and majority sentiment in Hungary; were it to threaten, I would emigrate.

13. Transnational processes are going forward in the world. In Europe, too, our continent's common, supernational consciousness has started to come alive. The adjective *European* has started to gain a sympathetic and real meaning. Such cultural reorganization is not foreign to Jews. Earlier on and in outstanding proportions, they tried to feel European.

In the decades since World War II, scattered folk anti-Semitism has not been elevated to the rank of national anti-Semitism in any country in Europe. If your instincts are alert, however, you can sense that the many kinds of aversions to Jews are connected somewhere in the atmosphere or underground.

The Jew who survived World War II cannot forget that they wanted to kill him. Jewish history consists of nothing but repeated epidemics of killing Jews. None was more justified or rational than any other.

There's more and more talk of the Jews themselves not being angels. The energy of Jewish organizations is periodically mentioned as a danger of catastrophic proportions. Why are they always bringing up Auschwitz? Others had their problems too; others, too, suffered a great deal.

The requisite for an ethnically pure nation has reappeared in Stalinist and extreme-right formulations. It is grand to be pure, unmixed, and homogeneous, having no more problems with minorities, having one language, one blood, one sacrifice, and of course one leader, the savior. If he's not here yet, he will come along and shout.

Increasing numbers of people think and say: We are no longer willing to feel guilty on account of the Jews. The atmosphere in the eastern half of Europe is a little murky. Many people do quite well under feudal socialism, even if they grumble, and they do not long for formal freedoms.

Those who prepared the public mood for the perhaps overly radical diminution of the Jewish population in their countries are being given increasingly eminent positions in their national pantheons. They were obsessed by their desire to solve the Jewish question, because they nurtured in themselves and in their environments the conviction that the Jews were the main cause and carriers of societal problems.

From there it is an easy intellectual leap to rehabilitate compassionately the radical anti-Semites; they always took their stand against subversive liberal individualism. On this not very spiritual road, it is difficult to stop before reaching the logical conclusion: the final solution.

The thirties have become the good old days; accordingly, the ideological fashions of that era have been ennobled.

1985

The Ethics of Self-Defense

14. Christians and Jews have not spoken openly enough to each other. The Christian-Jewish relationship consists of more than just ethnic-racial components, more than just sociocultural components. The foundation of the difference: two different notions of God. The rabbi from the ghetto—with his streml—understandably wasn't thrilled about the prospect of religious debate. It could result in his getting roasted.

15. The nationalist socialist "New Europe" experiment proved that mortal danger had not become obsolete. Both the Christian ministry and its theology were powerless against the ideology of the Third Reich, against persecution of Jews raised to the level of national law. The Judeo-Christian idea of solidarity among fellow men broke down. If prelates favor the passage of laws revoking citizenship for Jews, Christian churches may find in this abundant cause to undertake deep spiritual self-examination.

16. Our era does not favor deep spiritual self-examination. The flexible soul protests: "What about the Jews? You mean to say they're innocent? Are they such great democrats from the

Palestinian standpoint? If the victim is a criminal too, then we can say we have all committed crimes, then crime dissipates evenly, over our heads, up in the sky. Petty crime, major crime, it all amounts to the same thing. Spare us the oratory of self-accusation: we were enemies yesterday, today we are not, that's politics."

Everyone glorifies his own suffering; the weighing of sins should be entrusted to God. Classifying fellow men according to the severity of their sins is not the business of humans.

There is no solace for the death of our loved ones, just as there will be none for our own deaths, but the survivors visibly have been able to find consolation.

And the perpetrator has a surprising talent for looking back into the past and seeing himself as a victim too.

17. In the winter of 1944 we too could have hidden in Christian houses, with false papers as fake refugees from Transylvania, from localities already occupied by Soviet troops, telling doubters to get verification from the Soviets if they didn't believe us. But those doing identity checks simply tore up such documents and made the person get into line.

We could have paid someone to take the risk of harboring Jews, but we didn't do it. With one child of her own and four from relatives, my pretty young aunt said: I can't obligate myself eternally to someone for concealing us so we don't get killed. Why should we be killed? My aunt looked at us proudly, unsure of her next move. Indeed, why should we be killed?

18. There were more than two hundred Jewish children in my village, a separate elementary school and Talmud school. By the summer of 1945, only seven of us were still alive. The others had been suffocated.

In my eyes, the process of thinking and politics that ends by the gassing of my classmates is not freed of sin even retroactively. Every mentality complicit in the making of concentration camps deserves the same stigma.

I consider fraudulent any modern ethic not built on the absolute rejection of the world of the camps, of mass-produced murder.

19. How did we get here? we asked in houses marked by yellow stars, in ghettos and camps. We were the victims of a great mistake. In being careful not to be different, we lost ourselves.

We might have known we would not succeed in being truly one with the others. If we deny the promise of being different, we commit a crime against ourselves. Respect for the law, loyalty to the majority can only be conditional.

We wanted at least the appearance of similarity. Our denial of ourselves made us ridiculous, and it didn't help us. In approaching the majority peoples, the more common Jews were too pushy; they forced themselves on the hosts.

Our self-esteem crumbled, and we betrayed ourselves, obeying decrees that forced us out of the community of the living step by step. As punishment for bowing too deeply before the idols of nation, the Jews became helpless.

20. The foliage of my memories is not Jewish, but the roots are.

In the synagogue, I read the sacred text without understanding. My Cohenite father was invited up to the bimah to read the Torah. He made a circuit with the velvet-wrapped parchment scrolls containing the five books of Moses, copied by hand. When my father reached me with the scrolls on his arm, I too put my finger to my mouth. I touched the fringe of the velvet case.

The cantor sung on his platform, and the rabbi listened there. The parish chose the rabbi because of his learning, but he had no flock. The rabbi was a teacher, not a shepherd.

Devout young men, jabbering old men, scrambling little boys, we were only as saintly as each of us could manage. Some made business deals, some swapped marbles, some told jokes.

21. I do not keep kosher, and the mother of my older children is Christian. In high school, the rabbi failed me because I wore a hat. I had made it for myself out of the satirical newspaper, and wore it in front of the synagogue at Dohány Utca. In order to get a grade in religion, we had to go there every Friday afternoon. At the end of the service I sang with the others happily: Shema Yisrael, adonay elohenu, adonay ehod—Hear, O Israel, the eternal is one! We filed out of the boys' row of benches on the left in order to get closer to the girls filing out on the right. I was interested in a black-eyed girl with whom I had exchanged glances during the service.

I can mock my coreligionists or recoil from them; it doesn't matter, I'm still a Jew. We can use the language of any other nation, we can be citizens of any country, we can convert, become assimilated, connect our family to other cultural families. I can be Christian, Muslim, Buddhist, communist, it doesn't matter. The time will come when I see the Jew hiding inside me.

22. Anti-Semitism is a foolish sentiment, yet something causes it. The hosts didn't have an easy job. It's not easy to like something strange. It's not easy not to be afraid of it.

23. In Central and Eastern Europe there were more ethnic communities than nations. There were national scars and hatreds. Smaller nationalities wanted to be rid of the spiritual discomfort of being the latest to arrive. They all wanted a country of their own. And we could only observe passively, as we became residents of one country, then another, though we hadn't even stepped out of our houses.

24. Every one of my relatives in the ascending line was a Jew. My ancestors can be traced to the eighteenth century; they all lived in Hungary, in the county of Bihar. I never converted to another religion. I usually pray to the one and only God mutely, in Hungarian, or I just think of Him, outside of any language.

The deportation of my relatives from Hungary to Auschwitz was carried out on the basis of laws approved by Parliament. The Jewish laws enacted by Hungary under German guardianship during World War II made the civil rights of dozens of my relatives so profoundly dubious that they were denied even the right to live.

The majority of Hungarian citizens viewed this agenda indifferently, the next largest group approved of it, and only a small number turned against it in sentiment and deed. Sympathy for the human rights of our fellow men is a tender seedling in the Carpathian basin. If it's not me they're after, I'm better off lying low, says the average man. As long as the community reasons this way, almost anything can be done to it.

25. The Jews of Budapest pointed at the Jews of Sub-Carpathia: Look at the progress we have made on the road to assimilation, we are no longer like them. The young middle-class family was ashamed of the Orthodox grandfather. They were ashamed of his name, his pronunciation, and his murmuring of the blessing every time he washed his hands.

26. I was mainly ashamed that we, the Jews of Hungary, didn't fight. That we gave our lives without a battle. That we allowed ourselves to be steered without resisting. Had there been a ghetto uprising in Budapest like the one in Warsaw, I surely would have taken part. I was proud of my two cousins: one led a partisan detachment and the other joined an already existing group.

At the age of twelve I vowed that if this happened again, I too would have a weapon. If they came for me, I imagined, I would lie on the ground behind the front door to the apartment and open fire, I would shoot until I got hit, I wouldn't let them just lead me away.

And I would not permit them to lead me into a place where nothing mattered anymore, where I would be theirs. Where they could let the gas in from the ceiling and I would choke, duped and out of luck, beating on the door from the inside in vain, as I pictured it a thousand times. In my mind's eye I saw my cousins, girls younger than I, as they began to suffocate. I imagined their faces as their mouths stayed open. Today, when I see that in my mind's eye, I grit my teeth.

1985

Show Me Your Eyes

27. Which is more important? Our having been there, in Central Europe, or our having been more or less exterminated from there? A stubborn optimist like me believes that our presence was a more defining phenomenon than our annihilation. Or is that just the egocentrism of the survivor?

28. In all certainty, Jews found the geographical center of Europe an interesting place. It was possible to build wide-ranging networks of contacts from here; it was possible to move quite a bit of merchandise, to build factories and found banks.

Jews living in Hungary gladly became Hungarian. They took on the language and became comfortable with it. They wrote verse, philosophized, reported, wrote dissertations, did business, healed, acted, sang, joked, made love, argued, and prayed, all in Hungarian, and it quite quickly became natural for them to do so.

Others celebrate entry; we celebrate departure. There are places, however, Jews just didn't leave. With a stubbornness that went beyond the sensible, Hungarian Jews emancipated by the good offices of the liberal nobility clung to Hungary, with its variegated population. They participated wholeheartedly in building the country. They did not a little to help turn Budapest into a modern city.

It seemed there was a need for Jewish doctors and merchants, manufacturers and scientists, artists and artisans, entertainers and whores. Jews were the least willing to emigrate from Hungary. What was this unusual adherence not just to the country of the Danube and the Tisza but also to the host, the majority-Hungarian nation?

29. Fathers who study are continued in sons who study. Through two thousand years, the classroom was the Jews' temple. It is natural for the people of the written law to be good in school. Where emancipation was enacted, Jewish communities blossomed. Where success can be measured in abstract terms, Jewish boys and girls progressed well.

Those who are talked about a lot stand a good chance of being hated. The Jews were very concerned about what others thought of them, but they gave much less thought to themselves, their experiment in coexistence with the others, their own embourgeoisement. They hoped that the letter of the law would ensure equal rights for them.

It ensured them for a while, then no longer. If public pressure mounts, laws enacted yesterday may be taken out of force tomorrow, lawfully, within the framework of a state of law, and citizens with equal rights may be made into a pariah nation, a people of the barracks, wearers of striped clothes.

They believed in illusions, even though Jewish history prompts caution. Their alertness was average—in other words, inadequate. Liberal Jews forgot that the carnival of pogroms could be renewed with more advanced technology.

The warning was sounded only by the Zionists, and only they predicted that no one would protect the Jews if they did not do it themselves. The Zionists' warning proved prescient.

Many more Jews would have survived nationalist socialism

had there existed a country to receive them. In the 1930s, Hitler would have let the majority of them go, or put them on a boat. Primary responsibility for their mass annihilation lies with the murderers, secondary responsibility lies with those who handed them over, and tertiary responsibility lies with those who did not grant them asylum.

But if I do not consider us defenseless chattel, objects without souls, if on the contrary I regard us as the masters of our fate, then our own responsibility interests me much more than that of anyone else.

30. Within the Austro-Hungarian monarchy, on the territory of the Kingdom of Hungary, my Hungarian-speaking ancestors did not yet feel that they were only guests.

In the nation that existed before World War I, among Romanians and Serbs, Slovaks and Germans, Croatians and Ukrainians, Jews too could have equal rights. They could be what they wanted to be: Jews speaking Hungarian as their native language, Hungarians of the Jewish faith or converts to Christianity, Hungarian patriots, emancipated citizens of the Austro-Hungarian monarchy. They were Hungarians inasmuch as they were concerned and devoted members of that Central European cultural and political nation.

But after World War I, after the revolutions and counterrevolutions, in the Hungary reduced to a third of its size by the peace treaty of Trianon, we Jews—along with Gypsies—became unwelcome guests. We were forcefully reminded that we were "foreign to the nation." Earlier, we may have forgotten that we were not natives. Then we learned that the law was not our shield. One could proceed legally, using detailed decrees and regulations to wipe us off the face of the earth.

31. My uncles were officers of the joint (Austro-Hungarian) army, decorated several times over. Some of them were reckless,

played cards, caroused, sang, and played the violin, almost like provincial Hungarian gentlemen. I seem to recall that their behavior went both over and below the range of acceptable conduct for guests. It's not easy to blend resembling and differing in the just the right proportions. Living together tactfully requires lifelong study. One must learn the proper behavior for the traveler, the guest. More refined Jews tried to do something of the kind. In the process of adjustment, hurried assimilation was punished, as was obstinate isolation. Naturally, "refined" Jews also were punished for their balancing act.

32. After the war, my old Jewish religion teacher said: "Learn, my son, how the traveler should behave. The smart traveler has the wherewithal to give to others, to help care for children, the elderly, and the defenseless, anyone who joins him. He should be generous but reserved at the same time. He must not compete with the locals in their noisy revels. He should behave modestly with those who serve him, and give gifts to his hosts, but keep the ax within arm's reach. The heart of the traveler is not cheerful, because he senses trouble coming. He recognizes that in this place—where wine-fueled delirium made him believe he had a permanent shelter—he is foreign. He laughs a lot now, but he will suffer later. When he thinks clearly, he knows there are few people he can trust. He is obliging and careful with others; inside, he is firm and seeks the truth, and he never forgets the road is his home."

33. National emancipation in various countries did not stop the mutual dependence and coherence of clusters of Jews. They could not tell the truth, even if they believed their own intentions of becoming as Hungarian, German, or French as the others, remaining Israelites only by religion. They didn't tell themselves the truth either.

Total assimilation, either as an external demand or as a Jewish promise, was unrealistic. There was something fatefully stupid and demeaning in French and German Jews' shooting each other during World War I.

I watched my uncle with his signum laudis: in the summer of 1944 he went everywhere, unsuccessfully, to obtain papers giving him the status of exempted Jew. In the mirror of passing time, his gallantry was transformed into grotesque toadying.

Nolens volens, a connection came about between trying to fit in modestly and mass graves. Giving up Jewish consciousness was too great a price to pay for equal rights as citizens.

34. It doesn't matter what you think of yourself; you are a Jew, a destructive, harmful element; you do not belong among us, said the creators of the Jewish laws, first those passed at Nuremberg and then their epigones.

The oracles of the master and satellite nations said, Your assimilation is superficial and false; you will never be one with us. Neither your habits nor your style will ever be as rooted as ours. You were overconfident, you made yourselves rich, you wanted to surpass us. Perhaps yesterday assimilation was expected of you, but today we no longer even desire it.

To us, you are a question that must be answered. It would be easiest for you to leave. If you don't leave, the situation may deteriorate to the point where we may kill you. Wily Jews, do not lead us into temptation.

35. As soon as an increasing number of non-Jewish intellectuals believed that there was a "Jewish question" and that, moreover, it was the most important and urgent of all questions, arriving at the gas chamber was only a question of time, for it was logically consistent. Once the machinery of solution starts rolling, who will stop it short of the "final solution"?

The bishop submitting legislation to clamp down on Jews can

wash his hands clean in the afterworld too, for all it will help. That session of parliament remains in the annals. The legislators are forever enveloped by the stench of the crematorium. The preliminaries and the consequences are not separable.

36. The exilers called things by their names more sharply than the integrators. That the latter wrung their hands and accepted the romance of being victims was criminal negligence.

Auschwitz is there behind every Jew. It is not possible to wipe the slate clean of the purposeful extermination of children. One does not deny community with others who could have burned in the same oven.

One can count the corpses. Such bookkeeping does not console. They killed many more of us than the murderers among us killed.

The Germans found plenty of helpful partners among Austrians and Poles, Lithuanians and Ukrainians, Hungarians and Romanians, Croatians and Slovaks. The behavior of the majority of people indicated that they were unwilling to take any risk to help the Jews survive.

37. Several times now I have come across the view that Jewry's Central European adventure has come to an end. There is no Jewish community of significant size outside Hungary. Most recently, Jews were forced to emigrate from Poland in the late 1960s, proving that anti-Semitism disguised as anti-Zionism can be made into national policy in socialist countries too.

Many left Hungary as well, in different waves, but half of the Jews who survived World War II or were born afterward stayed here. There are practically no Jews in the countryside, but Budapest is home to the third largest Jewish community in Europe, after Moscow and Paris—almost one hundred thousand people, even more if we count half-Jews. Also, those who left come back to visit.

38. There would have been Stalinism in Eastern Europe even without Jews, but it is true that communist Jews were active in bringing the region into the socialist camp devised by Stalin. The relationship has soured since then; the emigration of Soviet Jews has begun. In the years following World War II, however, a not insignificant fraction of Jews who survived became tools of Stalin's policies, led by their own antifascist momentum.

There were also Jews who committed acts of cruelty as officers of the political police. It must be mentioned that there were plenty of Jews among the interrogated as well as the interrogators, but not even the most depraved of secret service agents resorted to exterminating children.

Where there were no longer any Jews, the new administrations were manned by non-Jews. Stalinism used many a Jew; at the same time, Jews were by no means indispensable.

In this neck of the woods, Jews are held responsible for capitalism and communism. The suffocation of my cousins, however, cannot be justified in retrospect either by capitalism or by the communism that succeeded the war.

39. Of the Jews in my village, the majority of men who survived did not choose the Communist path. Most left for Israel. Those who did join the Communist Party did the same work as before: they remained produce merchants or managers, only now they did so as the heads of state-owned corporations or collective farms. Others were just barely tolerated, as class aliens.

Some were deprived of their livelihood by national law. They moved to Budapest, took modest jobs in government, and tried to lie low. But in 1951, on a beautiful summer morning, a policeman hand-delivered an official relocation order—and they had to leave Budapest the same night. The order designated an unfamiliar village in the Alföld as their mandatory residence.

Pack your things, a truck will come around for the family

tonight, but leave everything except your most necessary belongings. Furniture, books, shirts were all used by the new residents and became their property. In those times one often heard the phrase: The old is replaced by the new.

40. Along the Danube in the past half-century there has been much fear and little cohesion. In our region, the dominant psychological habits are those of command and dependence; the culture of self-determination is sparse. The man in the street was not curious about the truth, and caution was championed in lofty phrases. In recent decades in Budapest, those who most emphatically pushed underground demonstrated the greatest degree of solidarity, even when it got them in trouble. And where something forbidden is being said, you are sure to find a few Jews.

There has always been a minority that came to the aid of their endangered fellow men, and the treasure of solidarity can be further enriched. Therefore, asserting we have no business being here in Central Europe is an unjust exaggeration.

41. There are enlightened citizens who do not hate the other person for being who he is.

Many Hungarian Jews have proved that they want to live here after all that's happened and feel no urge to declare themselves refugees. Sometimes a person of one of these impassioned minorities even tries to do something to make his city curious rather than suspicious of the other. He does good for his city by endeavoring to feel good in the spiritual skin of being different.

Perhaps a day will come when the Messiah glides past under our window and history speeds up. Then souls will come to life, strange convergences will become more frequent, routine will be broken, and every day will teach us something new. Then students will lock arms too tightly to be talked into splitting apart. A smile will fill the city and swallow the menace.

Perhaps a day will come when students progress more rapidly in the main subject at the school of humanity: understanding one another.

The unrecognized Messiah trudging along the Körút (Ring Road) with his faded suitcase will not care whether he touches the foreheads of Jews, Christians, or Muslims; he will be interested only in the story their eyes tell.

1985

Thoughts in Jerusalem

42. The Jews are a people whose nation lives in the state of Israel, while members of the ethnic group live all over the world. The existence of the Jewish nation was suspended for two thousand years, but in the twentieth century it has been renewed on the biblical land. The existence of the people itself was not suspended.

Zionism was a logical response in the era of nationalism. If a homeland is necessary at all costs, let us be a nation, Israel, the little America of Jews arriving from a hundred countries. If everyone wants to be a nation and not just a minority, then after two thousand years of being scattered about and excluded let us have a state of our own, so that we might defend ourselves.

If they can't stand us here, let us leave. Let us create a home with the tradition of the Holy Scriptures, so that not a single Jew has to feel like a tolerated newcomer with dubious rights. The Zionists had had enough of the assimilationists' self-delusions; they hoped they would be at home at the base of the Wailing Wall. They used the most remote past as justification to create a utopia.

The very first obligation of a person is to defend his life and the lives of his own. The goal of life is survival, and because that is not at all easy, life itself is a teleological task for the Jew.

You cannot awaken a guilty conscience in the anti-Semite. You can refer to Jesus, to democracy—it doesn't work. Hate is like a rock.

Whether a Jew is a Zionist or not, he must feel that the state of Israel has some connection to him too and puts him in a special light. He cannot avoid thinking he will go there if his present home becomes unsafe. And that notion is a source of guilt at the same time. Only then? Why only then? Diaspora Jews in Europe and America cannot escape this question.

43. He may speak any language, live anywhere and according to any customs: the Jew somehow does not succeed in permanently forgetting that he is a Jew. Jews' differentness remains even if Jews live the same way and in the same culture as their Christian friends. Jewish origin is always more dramatic than a mere dash of color in someone's cultural background.

I'm not a Jew, I am just of Jewish origin, says a Jew—in the company of Christians. Like a Frenchman of Russian descent, or a Hungarian of German descent. I'm not religious—he continues—I speak neither Hebrew nor Yiddish, I do not want to set myself apart from other people.

Behind his back, they call him a Jew. If for no other reason, then for the sake of objective truth and ease of expression. He cannot expect others to accommodate his mistaken idea about himself.

If he acknowledges being Jewish, it is more an acceptance of being different than an avowal of community with other Jews. It is not possible to lose this outsider status. That is our essence.

We wanted the elusive feeling of being at home, and we forgot to respect the outsider within us.

The others smiled conspiratorially behind our backs. We felt it in the short hairs on our neck, but we did not look back. Central European Jews had to or were expected to belong to too many state-national communities, one after the other. Each community wanted them whole, and if it could not swallow them, it spit them out.

The Jew is too strong in character, consciousness, tradition, and transcendence to be absorbed completely. For those who do not like to be different, being born a Jew is quite a burden. Those who simply like to be good patriots and those who like to stress their identity as Jews frequently will feel better in Israel. There at least they will not be hated for being Jews.

Being different is not shameful and not unpleasant, unless we imagine that every proper person must belong body and soul to one national community. The majority of Jews, too, prefer to do as the majority does.

If, however, I have come to accept being different from the others, then being a Jew is no longer a daunting step.

Even if a Jew is utterly like his environment, even if he has learned everything that can be learned of the surrounding peoples' culture, he still remains somehow different. It is impossible in principle for Jews to become completely assimilated into another national environment, no matter how far-reaching or spectacular that assimilation is.

44. If you read the Old Testament, you come to understand that the greatest value is survival, survival as a Jew. Jewish transcendence is nothing other than the undertaking of this uncomfortable task. The obligation to survive as a Jew is concomitant with the requirement of elevated existence.

Existence burdened by God: this is the gift and the calamity of the Jews. This is the source of the radicalism that propels Jews across the frontiers of a given reality, and that ejects them from consensus within their own community as well. A Jew is someone who doesn't want simply to be but, rather, to serve as the fulfillment of the obligation imposed by God.

The here and now, full of suffering: this is utopia. Life sanctified by the law, possible anywhere. May your country come! Let the emissary of the Lord sit down at this table! This child could be the redeemer.

If life can be sanctified, then earthly life is not a vale of tears. If salvation is a permanent job, then existence is not a disaster. One must learn the divinely inspired mode of existence. By the end of a full life we tire, but death is not yet the golden gate to heaven; it is, rather, the nothing and nowhere granted by the mercy of the Almighty.

Some say the Messiah visits and possesses everyone momentarily. Some say the Messiah on the donkey will never come. He might come by train, and no one will be waiting at the station.

45. My father followed the tradition; he handed me over to my destiny as a Jew by having me circumcised. Circumcision of the genital organ substitutes for circumcision of the heart; the name of the deed is covenant. The father wants his son to do as he does, to try to live a life on God's terms.

We derive our laws and our personal decisions from our covenant with God, not from blood and not from the earth but from religion. Not territory or language or state makes the Jew a Jew, it is done exclusively by the covenant. Ten commandments and the flight of the stork, that's what I saw in my childhood if I lifted my gaze from the breakfast table.

46. The Jews forbid themselves the pictorial representation of God, but the Scripture itself is an image. God can be represented and approached in an infinite number of ways. Everyone translates the unapproachable into his own daft vision. If it makes you feel better, visualize a calf, a bull, a deer, an eagle, or even a

human figure, a group of acquaintances forever having fun and quarreling. Call divine the self-sacrificing young prophet or the young prince who leaves his family, wanders, and gains great wisdom in the course of his long life. Say that His most credible interpreter is the experienced, wily camel herder.

But say all this only for lack of anything better, because when you look within yourself, you know God's every face is but a mask, a reflection on a shard of glass. Compared to the infinity of God, Moses and Jesus, Buddha and Muhammad are just protagonists of novels.

47. I could honestly convert to all existing faiths in turn and browse through the God market as a world-traveling metaphysical wanderer. But I don't have time for interior monologue, or to split hairs with priests, who have no more and no less inside information than, say, my high school teachers.

No, I have absolutely no need of spiritual leaders. I need books and friends. I am not at all a believer. I'm not even a believing Jew. I do not believe the Torah and the prophets, I just read them. I should believe the Song of Songs? The brooding reflections of Ecclesiastes? I believe my son—with a single shriek he signals whether he wants something or not.

I know the majority of priests do not affect piety. I have friends among them, but conversation with them has never yet motivated me to put theology ahead of poetry, the mystique that is secular and that can be cynical too.

In Jerusalem, it was splendid to amble from a temple of one religion to one of another, and to observe the servants of God in their various uniforms. I felt as if a costume shop had come to life around me.

48. In Jerusalem, on the street or on the bus, I was often seized by a visual sensation of being at home: I felt these faces were

deeply familiar. I liked the way children danced on the street or were rowdy in the synagogue. I got the feeling that the whole thing is for the children. The Jewish cult of the child can even be viewed as sentimentality; it is justified by the satisfied children that come to mind. When my cousin pampers her grandchildren, perhaps she is also thinking of the daughter taken to the gas chamber. Children are very important here; adultery is not in fashion. Husband and wife stay together; spouses have more esteem for each other here than in other cultures. There are norms here that regulate life; three-thousand-year-old norms have been re-created, and they continue.

Eating kosher in Jerusalem means only that I don't seek out treyf; I do not go to the Jaffa Gate, to the Christian Palestinian butcher to buy pork chops. It's easier for me to eat kosher in Israel, and it even tastes good. In the course of our stay here, we ate many more vegetables and much less meat.

The religious holidays have become folk holidays. You can berate the rascals and idiots on television, because it's normal for a Jew to enjoy sharpening his tongue on idiots and rascals. But you can be sure of one thing: as a Jew here, you are not defenseless.

I know I will miss Jerusalem painfully, this blueness and this whiteness, the sharp outlines of things.

The Israeli Jews made a nation, with the institutions of modern life, with infrastructure and architecture on a grand scale; they maintained it and defended themselves. They live in a lively democracy that cannot be transformed into dictatorship. I myself remain a Jew of the Diaspora, but I place part of my being here. I am glad that I have cousins in Israel. My acquaintances here are not depressed by public lies or by the fear of attacking public lies. They have other problems, ones that are quite weighty; that is what makes them sad.

49. We closed the circle of sacred concepts too quickly. We oversimplified sanctity to a technique of living. I do not wish to

feel such anxiety about eating, clothing, and everyday habits. I eat what there is, what tastes good to me. I wear ordinary European clothes, as do most people in the world by now.

I apportion my time so that I do not have to separate the sacred and the profane. The time in which I write, or walk my son, or talk to my friends, is sacred. The time in which I participate in my wife's enthusiasm about how much our son already knows, or about how delicious these sour cherries are, is also sacred. It is precisely as sacred as it is profane, and as profane as it is sacred.

I have become accustomed to considering observations of propriety parenthetical. What am I allowed and not allowed to eat? I listen to neither the doctor nor the rabbi. In my manner of dress and my hairstyle, I pay little attention to fashion or religious prescriptions. I like a dark-gray tweed jacket and dark-gray flannel trousers. The shirt should be white or light blue. I do not wear a tie or earlocks.

All religions aim to obligate their faithful to certain habits and certain holidays; I consider that a cultural-historical fact. I stand perplexed by the religious state built not on existing Jewish society but, rather, on three hundred sixty commandments, the collected laws of the Torah, interpreted by the rabbis.

In Israel, and all over the world, there are many Jews not willing to submit their lives to the judgment of theologians interpreting text, nor are they willing to give up separation of church and state. The liberty of the citizen is in danger when the affairs of politics and religion get mixed up. In every community—among Jews too—the half-baked speak loudest. Jews expel other Jews from the community.

If fundamentalism comes to power in Israel, there won't be much traffic between Israeli and Diaspora Jews. Then we will be without support, and they will be isolated.

The Jews need Israel, Israel needs the Jews. Without the support of world Jewry, Israel is less secure in the Middle East. But as a Diaspora Jew, I also have support behind me, in the form of a country that will take me in if I go there, not on the basis of an individual judgment or out of mercy but because I have a right to it, according to the founding law of the state.

50. Jews too have a tendency to concentrate on the narrower issue, the national, the internal affairs of the state of Israel, the struggle of various Jewish religious denominations, of religious and worldly Jews to shape the spirit of the nation, and of the modern interpretation of numerous parts of the Talmud. In the eyes of the outsider, these matters all seem like recondite anthropological fixations rather than dilemmas of metaphysical import.

Jews are incapable of blithely separating life and religion. For Jews, this life is a task to be sanctified, not a temporary unpleasantness but, rather, a framework that must be filled in. The not sanctified is suspicious, however. That which is not sacred is unclean.

Allowed/not-allowed clauses, prescriptions, prohibitions, and hair-splitting in such abundance, are they not signs of an anxious soul? The people of the law are prone to the weakness of making themselves vulnerable to the explainers of the law. There are ghetto walls that others build around the Jews, and there is a ghetto wall that the Jews themselves build.

51. What is my Jewishness if it is not religion, not traditional community, and not return to the land of Israel? I met people in Israel who think those of us who stayed in Central Europe have basically made a mistake. According to them, we live in a state of deficient self-esteem, in self-deceit. Sticking around in the neighborhood that contained the camps is akin to giving up, to surrendering.

I too have asked myself: What is this stubbornness in me? Why don't I wish to move permanently far from the doorway where they almost shot me down? Perhaps it is also important that a few blocks from that door I was later a young newlywed.

I do not look anywhere for my mystical "mother's lap" homeland. The existence of distance between myself and others I find not tragic or even saddening. Wherever I have been up to now, I have found satisfactory conversation partners. Perhaps I will be punished someday for being the provocation that I am. That will be then.

I prefer being hunted to being the hunter, but I am not caught easily. Maybe it's characteristically Jewish to sees things the way I do. But when I look in the shaving mirror, it doesn't even cross my mind that I am looking at a Jew.

52. In my interpretation, Jewishness means the imperative of personal freedom of thought. The task of a Jew in Central Europe is to be an adult. Ancient and much attacked peoples, experienced in survival, have an outstanding chance at adulthood.

Living in a diaspora, scattered about, means that we can stand on our feet in small groups, or even alone. I have always felt a person in a group is unfinished goods. The typical community: a nursery school. The person who is as he should be according to type is a little obnoxious to me.

I am able to follow the reasoning of several types of nationalism, but I do not espouse any of them. I am a person; every narrower definition is incidental and therefore questionable.

The longing of the Jews to find a community is moving but unachievable. In Israel, they have succeeded in being lonely as a nation.

53. The Jews' greatest virtue is their greatest crime in the eyes of the anti-Jewish: they manifest somewhat more solidarity toward one another than toward other peoples. Now that the danger of extinction is not at the threshold, this solidarity must bridge ever

greater distances. There is growing estrangement between those
living inside Israel and those living outside, between the religious and the secular, the hawk and the dove, those in favor of
isolation and those in favor of cohabitation, between fundamentalist and pluralist Jews.

Pluralism is not a foreign idea to Jews. Without a doubt, the
range of diversity among Jews is wider than among other nations.
Almost every language, culture, societal position, physical type,
and political aim finds its representatives among us.

It is a fact, however, that Jewry has its own fundamentalism,
just like other peoples. It has religious and nationalist fundamentalism; both regard diversity as an error and individual freedom
as a weakness of the community.

The various nationalist fundamentalisms are quite similar to
one another, even if they stress the uniqueness of their own
essence. Ironic but inescapable: nationalist rhetoric is the most
international of intellectual products.

54. The strongest argument for Jewish fundamentalism is the
anti-Jewish fundamentalism of other nations. As soon as European Christian fundamentalism and then nationalist fundamentalism destroyed the greater part of European Jewry, Near
Eastern Islamic fundamentalism appeared, with its focus and
common basis: anti-Zionism.

Can a pluralist response be made to a fundamentalist attack?
Islamic fundamentalism will probably be a lasting phenomenon,
not a passing fashion. It is a worldview that aims to conquer; it of-
fers unity and demands radical conversion. The most obvious response: only stubbornness can wrestle with stubbornness. Every
blow should be avenged by a counterblow. Convince them they
won't get far by force of arms. If you aren't hard, they will be.
They respect only those who can strike back.

If the Jews were not able to strike back, if they were vulnerable to their opponents' weapons, then their opponents would say the same thing the Germans said: "We don't want to kill the Jews or drive them into the ocean, we just want them to leave here. They should go back where they came from! It's all the same to us where they go, let them go to Europe or anywhere that will take them in!"

The situation of an Arab is different from that of a Jew. There are twenty Arab countries but only one Jewish country. The Palestinians can obtain total autonomy, even from the Israeli right. But they will not be granted national-military self-determination as long as Islamic fundamentalism wants not only the reestablishment of the pre-1967 borders but also the disappearance of the "Zionist entity" from the Middle East.

The occupied territories can lead only to territorial obsession on both sides of the conflict. There are presently irresolvable differences. Two nationalisms want the same land.

Maybe the Arabs and the Jews will live beside each other in peace when they both get tired? Maybe the Jews will tire before the Arabs? Neither will tire. There will be many more deaths, but neither side will give up. Perhaps eventually they will realize that in their antagonism they have grown accustomed to each other.

55. Who can judge which murder is proper and which is improper? When Jewish airplanes carry out retaliatory attacks against an Arab village, which woman's death is proper and which is improper? Which young man unquestionably had to be killed? Which stone-throwing child must be shot?

If we could rewind time and get to know any of the people who are now corpses, which killing would be deemed proper by the person who skims the news and indifferently approves the retaliatory strike? Reprisal is necessary in general, says the stalwart man on the street; there's no reason to spend a lot of time on the identity of the victims. They shoot, we shoot, it's that easy.

The hero of our period: the superficial person who devotes only as much time to news of brutality as it occupies on television news broadcasts. People need the excitement that accompanies the repetition of silliness. They like to be frightened and to get angry.

56. The Israeli Jews worked a lot. They made a country in which there is no penury, where alert democracy restrains nationalist fundamentalisms, where people can say what they think, where the Jews have become normal citizens.

I see my relatives and former acquaintances now stand up straight. I see, compared to them, the unsureness of Budapest Jews who secretly sneak down here for visits, with visas issued in the West, and ask me not to mention our meeting here when we get back to Hungary.

The Israelis accept themselves as they are; their aura is more refreshing because of it. The majority of Hungarian Jews do not accept themselves as Jews, and there are some who make their role as minority Jew into an unhealthy fixation. Those who live not as subjects but only objects of their fate will be neurotic sooner or later.

57. If there is any meaning to the concept of a chosen people, it is this: solidarity. A people is chosen to the extent that it shows solidarity. There is solidarity in the slaughterhouse only if the cattle attack the butcher. Only if they break out of the slaughterhouse.

It is not enough for me to refrain from doing unto others as I would not be done by them. I must sometimes also do unto others as I would be done by them. I must sometimes save others. Personal responsibility is not waived in the course of any type of ritual obedience to rules, whether the obedience is in the form of practicing yoga or a series of symbolic acts.

Jewish sense of family is often mentioned. It can be suffocat-

ing, but it also means that Jewish parents give somewhat more to
their children than the usual.

Sometimes there is no stopping on the road of sacrifice, and
we have to give up everything, even our own lives, for those
close to us.

Those who acted that way did not consider all the options;
rather, they did what had to be done. If a person does his job, the
final hour may strike, but it will find him sitting in the sun, cheer-
fully and without regrets.

58. I walk through the Rehavia in Jerusalem, the affluent quarter of hillside villas similar to those in Budapest and Berlin.
Central European intellectual-bourgeois architecture, two- and
three-story condominiums, stone walls, balconies. Around the
yards are pine and willow trees, but palms and oranges as well.
Everything is familiar, the durable good taste of the 1930s and
1940s. The people remade here what they left behind.

My cousin lives here with her pharmacist husband. They will
not be taken to camps from here. No one will pull this little girl
from her mother's arms out of sheer goodness, so that mother
and child should not be led together into the gas chamber. These
teachers, doctors, businessmen, and officials will not go humbly
in through the gate of the death camp. Here, they have security,
they behave naturally.

At the end of the 1940s, 600,000 Israeli Jews welcomed 900,000
Jewish refugees, mainly from Arab nations, which suddenly expelled them. The citizens of the new state, many of whom lived
in tents, decided that the Jewish state would have legitimacy only
if it accepted every Jew who wanted to go there. Otherwise there
was no sense in speaking of national solidarity.

59. When Jews abandon the imperatives and prohibitions of
their own religion, they tend to search for a new faith, a comprehensive life strategy. What is religion but a comprehensive life

strategy for the individual and the community? We might say that Jews are faith-hungry. They want to be sure of the rightness of their actions. Compared to a non-Jewish environment, in Israel there is less of the realism that expresses itself as wallowing in the morally dubious. We either negotiate with the Almighty or we deny His existence. If we deny it, we promptly fabricate another god-likeness for ourselves.

We give up divine transcendence? Then let there be human transcendence! Then let there be scientific transcendence! A new religion founded by a lapsed Jew: scientific socialism. It spread like the ideas of heretic Jewish preachers about the god who became a man.

Among nonreligious Jews, sociological and economic concepts were lifted to the rank of religion, theoretical texts were granted the validity of revelations. Nonreligious Jews were able to attribute vital significance to new structural definitions of the universe and human consciousness. They became entangled in progress, of both the patiently enlightening and the impatiently revolutionary variety. If conservatism is in vogue, they are more radically conservative than anyone else.

There are many strict or sarcastic minds among Jews; they cast moral blame on those who disagree with them. On the other hand, it is an unruly and stubborn race: nonconformists, dissidents, people who think differently, heretics, freethinkers, avant-gardists, degenerates, destroyers of unity, seducers, and tempters all grow in Jewish society, like mushrooms after rain.

You can throw the prophet into the well, you can burn him, nail him to the cross; he is so stubborn, so obdurate, that he will die rather than take back what he has said. He preaches dangerous ideas, he undermines the solid foundations of the state.

The paradox Jews carry within themselves is what makes them so stimulating and unsettling: they are capable of both radical affirmation and denial of the law, simultaneously. Jews have a passionate relationship with the law; they want it and oppose it, they worship it and exploit it. They want to put all of life under the authority of the law; at the same time, however, they want to be liberated from all authority. The law is so important for the Jew because it is not just the regulator of relationships but also the quest for salvation.

60. At the end of the twentieth century, in the sixth millennium, it is fairly anachronistic, fairly provocative of us to explain and justify our civil and national situation by referring to God. The Arabs do it as well; that's why the Middle East is so chaotic. We might say that God drives humans crazy: He whispers different things to everyone.

61. As I looked over the titles of writings and lectures in Jerusalem, it seemed that world culture there was interesting mainly from the standpoint of relevance to Jewishness. Some people become more Jewish after a visit to Israel, some become less so. Nationalism grows more tolerable as it gets older and more able to laugh at itself.

Today's Israeli nationalism does not laugh at itself. It is convinced that "we are the best" and that those others, the opponents, are very bad. Which people wouldn't be driven crazy by the idea of being God's people?

Those few texts, ideals, traditions we possess are the source of all truth, the sum of all values. A kind of nationalist-religious fundamentalism is emerging, an uncompromising Jewish particularism that does not approve of the universalism of the European Jew.

I frequently perceived a general sense of grievance by Israelis against Christian and Islamic cultures. It creates a sort of Jewish autism. There is too much complaining that the others were always bad to us, too much self-pity. In company, during dinner, older people tell their concentration camp stories again and again.

Rehashed self-pity is accompanied by a kind of arrogant enjoyment, not as enjoyable for the listener. Especially irritating are young American Jews when they claim moral superiority over other communities by using the authority of the Holocaust, when they boast of the suffering of others—suffering that they, young American Jews, did not experience.

62. Not the least of the many awful effects of the Holocaust is that it becomes a sacral event of pathetic recollected consciousness. To refer to it using unauthorized language is forbidden. Comparable human suffering does not exist and cannot be imagined. The whole of Jewry is elevated by it. Moral preeminence based on suffering bears examining.

Holocaust rhetoric became official phraseology in Israel, the chief legitimizer of national existence, of personal arrival there and immigration policy; it even appears to validate the annexation of the West Bank in the eyes of many Jews. It seems more and more insulting to argue that the death of Jewish children in the gas chamber does not validate the bombing of Palestinian camps in Lebanon, another action that causes the death of children.

A persecuted minority founds a nation, becomes a majority, and starts to oppress the local Arab inhabitants or those who have emigrated from neighboring countries, who in turn discover and experience the same belated nationalism as the Jews.

Only rhetoric makes the conflict of neighboring peoples grow into a life-or-death struggle. Rhetoric can also spoil the coexistence of peaceful civilians.

63. The Israeli Jews wanted a state, they wanted to be like other nations. They revived the Hebrew language and locked themselves inside. They applied themselves to nationalist archaeological excavations, to prove that they had always been

there. Even their architecture is nationalist, intended to demonstrate a kind of superiority.

They gave up being cosmopolitan, being rootless, without territory, and therefore they lost something of value. Hardly anyone loved European culture more passionately than the Jews. The quality of being different can be lost; the Jewish state too can have a nationalist, inwardly turned culture, thus resembling other provincial cultures.

64. If this new community stakes its identity chiefly on its opposition to others, the strongest unifying bond will be war. Not religion, not culture, not memories, but, rather, defending oneself with arms. If the Jews give the military such prominence, they will undoubtedly be good soldiers, that is, they will conquer. It's just that conquering is bad for the conqueror. Occupied territories always spoil the occupier. Occupation leads to the special interests of the national religious community superseding human rights and humanist universalism.

Nationalism can do nothing else; it is hostile to the neighbors, it justifies its aggression against others, it places military virtues above civil virtues, it encourages the feeling of superiority to other peoples, and sees the essence of the nation in combat.

65. A strange intellectual eddy: the inability to think of anything but local-national affairs and grievances. Everything in the press and the bookstores is about them. If the world rejects Israel's occupation of Arab territories, then the Israelis reject the world. Resentment rules the conversation. This narrowed state of consciousness is accompanied by belief in one's own absolute moral discernment and a tendency to accuse others.

When I visit Tel Aviv, Hungarian Jews who have lived in Israel for a long time immediately ask me: If I'm a dissident, why don't I emigrate? Hungarians accepted Nazism and then Stalinism, they say.

But Jewish communists also played a part in Stalinism, I note.

Even the East Germans didn't hang people in the 1950s, only the Hungarians did, says my partner in argument.

Yes, Rákosi and his bunch. The Russians used them, and when those Hungarians finished the dirty work, the Russians dumped them. After World War II, some young Hungarian Jews with internationalist illusions became naive instruments of Stalinism.

In 1945, many young Jews accepted jobs with the political police, thereby entrusting themselves to the logic of events, which dragged them further. First they beat fascists, so they believed, then all kinds of hostile elements, with Jews among them in good number. The Jews who loudly demonstrated their anti-Russianness in the 1980s ought not to have forgotten this.

66. I would call the spiritual wall that divides Jewish and Christian society a ghetto. Not to have contact with each other, not to marry each other, not to trust each other, not to open up to each other.

The other person is worthy of respect regardless of his country of citizenship, national origin, skin color, or religion. To hurt someone because of these attributes is ugly.

Every nationalism is accompanied by a bunch of prejudices—contemptuous, unfriendly, suspicious, and hostile prejudices against one group or another. One hostile nation can only presume bad things about the other, and it pays the price by having all its thoughts and spiritual energy tied down by continuous resentment.

67. In Central Europe, in Hungary, there are anti-Semites around me in good number. Enemies you can find anywhere. Especially if you are a Jew. Those who have nothing better to do than hate me can find plenty of reasons to do so. I have almost got used to this state of affairs. Among those who think about me,

the minority that hates me will mention my being a Jew in larger proportions from now on. I should consider that unbearable, a reason to leave Hungary?

European anti-Semitism today is not getting ready to slaughter the Jews. That would be beyond its means. Fanatic Muslims living in the countries surrounding Israel dream of bloodier acts. The proportion of fanatics in a nation is always small. Sometimes, however, they use strictness and adulation and succeed in infecting their whole environment.

They don't like us? Fine. It's their business, not mine. I aspire neither to lead them nor to be in their good graces.

I would leave my homeland only if folk anti-Semitism was raised to the level of state anti-Semitism.

It's hard not to have mixed feelings about Jews. We are a combative people. I'm leaving here, leaving Israel. Too many Jews here. I'm starting to think we are the only ones who have suffered in this world, that only we exist in this world.

My partners in conversation, like Hungarians at home, are not really interested in what happens in other parts of the world. We Jews are really interested only in ourselves. If others do not lock me into my Jewishness, should I lock myself?

In long conversations, evening after evening, the only topics are local events. True, there is plenty to talk about, tempers are always flaring.

What fantastic egocentrism—a piece of land as tiny as the West Bank, the right bank of the river Jordan, the territory formerly belonging to Jordan, presently under Israeli military administration, spoken of in the plural but not bigger than a Hungarian county, though Hungary is tiny enough itself. I have never thought so much about so little land.

Affairs temporarily impervious to solution. They will be treatable only if the Arabs and the Jews learn to coexist, if both parties recognize the special opportunities offered by living together, if both get tired of searching for exclusive solutions, if each reluctantly adjusts its worldview to the other a little, perhaps even its religion.

These Middle Eastern peoples have a tendency to stick out their chests. Their culture serves this conceit. One should guard against it, suggesting that they are not alone in the house, they are not alone in the history of the world.

A better use of culture would be to cool down this miserable, bulging, arrogant, boastful, expansive, pushy self, the one that screams louder than others and pushes them aside. Culture should discipline the self and force it to formulate thoughts precisely.

68. Fascism, which has many variations and thus emerges throughout the world again and again, is really just extreme nationalism—with absolute power. The state in this case becomes a public prosecutor. Killing of Jews is not the main distinguishing feature of fascism. A more essential element is the nationalist cult of the state and the military, the one-party system, deification of the ruler, omnipotence of the political police, and institutionalized discrimination.

The ruling political team spots a societal group within the borders, preferably one with strong ties to the outside. The group is demonized, then criminalized. The ruling team declares it an enemy and persecutes it. Identifying a minority glues the majority together.

Without a doubt, however, Jews are exceptionally suited to assume the role of official enemy in all kinds of fascism. Their external connections make the extent of their internal commitment questionable. They are the most likely to hesitate to submit entirely to the local authorities. They do not believe completely in the local wisdom, they do not share completely in the local prejudices.

As soon as the people's hate is in your hands, the people are in your hands. When the nation lays its hate down at the feet of the chief, it puts a leash around its own neck and gives the end to the leader. The leader can be a fly-by-night nobody, a demagogue with grandiloquent language who is not yet in power but has the gift of directed and obsessive hatred.

The Jews were a handy target for numerous variations of fascism. Without anti-Semitism, Hitler could not have got such a hold on the Germans. If there are no Jews, or if Jews can no longer be nominated for the role of official enemy, then another group will do, but fascism must have an official internal enemy. The ruling party—with the chief at its fore—must be worshiped; the infiltrating enemy, the fifth column, must be hated. It is not even necessary for a nation to be fascist for such a dim-witted Manichaeism to come to dominate its consciousness.

69. In the second half of the 1950s, a new system was inaugurated, and the rhetoric of class struggle filled the air. With my adolescent head, I was an onlooker, I did not want to participate in it. For one, it was impossible not to notice that this battle too was being fought against me. Against another of my names this time. Against another of my traits: my bourgeois nature.

I made an effort to remain objective in this particular class struggle. I wanted to understand the people around me, whom I found uninformed and misled rather than originally malevolent. The treatment given the poor by the rich in the previous regime had also been class struggle. The poor were kept in humiliating poverty and coldly exploited. Now the tables were turned, the hour of revenge for the poor had arrived.

Every new encroachment or unpleasantness elicited a nod from me—turnabout is fair play. Yes, it actually makes sense that they exclude me from their universities, I said, when they excluded me.

70. I wanted to broaden myself rather than narrow myself. I did not want to snuggle into any kind of ritual community. I didn't dance the Communist dance about the rumbling train, just as I didn't dance the original with the Zionists. Not a scout, I was repulsed by every kind of scouting.

I did not want to submit myself to various artificial rules for living in order to differentiate myself from the majority and bond myself with a very few people. I was not willing to give moral significance to the question of writing on a Saturday, or eating a ham sandwich. The fascists killed equally those who kept kosher and those who ate treyf. Moreover, by being so conspicuous, the Orthodox Jew paralyzed himself, became unsuitable for the underground, incapable of hiding, and thus made himself even more vulnerable to the machinery of genocide. Everyone knew that those who had chosen assimilation had more ways to survive, because they had Christian friends. The more conservative a Jewish community—my village, for example—the less possible it was to save particular members of it.

Many young Jews felt their parents' truths were no longer valid. Young Jewish men returned from forced labor abroad and no longer wore earlocks or beards, caftans or hats. They slipped out of the religious uniform. They said they would no longer voluntarily wear distinguishing badges.

71. This sentence is proper, that other one is improper. The majority of people try to avoid saying something improper. They would rather say nothing. The smartest thing to do in a dangerous dictatorship is to play dumb. The suspect is always shifty, doesn't know, hasn't heard about it, doesn't remember, never believed that; the suspect doesn't think anything about anything. The discouraging thing about this gray camouflage is that after a while a person actually becomes gray.

Of the experience I have acquired, I must keep something secret. There are so many kinds of ideological censorship: fascist and Communist, religious and national; collective sensitivities show an unparalleled talent for resentment. You must be careful of what you say and to whom you say it. Even the walls have ears; you don't know what's going on next door. The things you don't say can't cause trouble.

Communism was a good lesson after fascism. One says nation, the other says class, but in both we must be very careful about the things we say, because a rash sentence can mean trouble.

72. In my youth, I didn't like the way older people transformed past events into sentimental mythology, almost proudly. Conversation always curved back to indulgent self-pity. I felt there was a strange kind of hedonism in this stubborn repetition.

Following a change of regimes, the lengthy recounting of insults, oppression, and frustrations suffered in the past becomes a general spiritual habit anyway; in all likelihood, it is the soul's delayed defense, its reaction to memories of being humiliated. The more you suffered, the more special you are. The more promising your career. Years followed in which past suffering was turned into merit. A gaudy catalog of former injuries and losses was a way for some people to get access to privileges. Moving biographical examples of the misery of the day laborer or the urban proletariat opened the path upward on the societal ladder.

I started to feel that everyone had suffered horribly under the previous regime. Then the same thing happened with those persecuted under Stalinism. A little persecution under a Communist regime raised a person's value in the West or in unofficial public opinion at home; some actually become saints or oracles by virtue of having been persecuted. The former prisoner can talk the most incredible rubbish; he has a right to it, he has suffered a lot. Years in prison draw a halo around the heads of many a donkey.

The ritual of transformations: the formerly persecuted obtain power and silence the complaints of others. There are officially appreciated complaints and improper complaints. In the atmosphere of revenge, the loser's complaint only vexes. The victor's retrospective complaint is elevated. The differentiation between suffering that deserves sympathy and suffering that should be ignored is a question of politics.

73. The majority of Germans and Hungarians took no part in the persecution of Jews. They were little people; no one asked them what should happen to the Jews. The great majority of the people in this Central and Eastern European region was presented with faits accomplis.

I hated those who passionately accused others, when the accusers were anti-Semites; I should like them now that they're Jews or Communists? Now the mocking prosecutors shake their fingers before another packed jury.

The concept of collective sin, of general condemnation of communities, was repulsive to me. A criminal race? A criminal religion? A criminal nation? A criminal class? I saw individuals, not collectives.

In any case, I was relocated from the category of alien-national and member of a criminal race to the category of class alien or, rather, class enemy. I won't say from a rock to a hard place, because this time they didn't want to kill me. If this label wears off, another will come; so be it.

If I call to mind people who were good to me and those who were bad to me in the past decades, neither group can be characterized as Jewish or non-Jewish. Jews and non-Jews are represented in both groups. The functionaries who censored me from public culture were Jewish. To me, that satisfactorily proves the exaggerated nature of beliefs about complicity among Jews.

As I recall, I was a thorn in the side of not just the zealous Jewish militant Communists but, ironically, also the zealous Jewish militant anti-Communists. And not just the Jewish ones of either group.

Many people don't appreciate an autonomous person who refuses to accept ideological sentimentality or the notion that some must be loved very much while others must be hated very much. This kind of autonomy was stamped "aristocratic" in the 1950s. It was one of the recurring justifications in my various expulsions. You do not belong among us, said a kind young girl warmed by Party membership, in her otherwise poorly heated house on the outskirts of town. You're most probably right, I said. She was genuinely angry that I was not devastated by her statement.

Every generation has many searching souls. A significant portion of postwar searchers found the Party membership book and pressed it to their breasts. Now they will perhaps be born-again Christians or Jews, or they will swear allegiance to the national flag daily, possibly with a mandatory morning ritual, like American schoolchildren. The wave will hit the obstinate as well, and even if it doesn't sweep them away, it will crash so wildly that they will be left gasping for breath.

1986

Deus Semper Maior

74. I believe that every person is divine, but I don't believe that any person is God. Without honest dialogue between Judaism and Christianity, neither can be a truly personal religion, neither can renew itself enough to become more than a tradition to be respected, more than just teaching—neither can become a living way of thought as well.

There is no Catholic universality without the universality of Jewish monotheism. However, a Judaism that remains within ethnic-national borders, without the further elaboration of Christian ethics, tends toward formalism.

If I remove from Christianity the somber grandeur and realism of the Jewish foundation, the remaining part easily becomes dogmatic or pietistic.

Three-quarters of the Scriptures are common to Jews and Christians. The remaining one-quarter, the text of the Christian New Testament, is also the work of Jewish authors. The Jews can thank Christianity for their sacred books' becoming the most widespread collection of text in the world. We can be grateful to Christianity for spreading the Ten Commandments across the globe. For this very reason we should think long and hard about accepting the Sermon on the Mount as our own as well.

75. The fate of Jesus is the personal illustration of Jewish fate. Biblical Jewry made a special covenant with God. The evangelical Jesus refers in several ways to his own special covenant with the Father. Jeshua of Nazareth encourages humility in one sentence, in the next says he comes from the house of the Father. Perhaps he just wanted to say that we are all God's children.

He was surely tempted by the thought that it was just he, he alone. Neither a nation nor a person will have an easy life believing—and making no secret of believing—that it or he is closer to the Father than others are. The meeker ones accept the individual's superiority, the prouder ones do not: the most they are willing to acknowledge is the oligarchy of divine inspiration.

In Jesus's time, proud young Jews were crucified by the thousands for thinking themselves prophets and asserting that they knew more than the others, for suggesting that they were the only ones who really knew the will of the Almighty. It is a Jewish habit to know almost everything better than the others. Mindful of his haplessness in this world, what else can the prophet do but castigate, rebuke, threaten, and console the others in the name of something higher, in the name of the highest of all?

76. Christianity was established by a radical minority: Jewish dissidents scattered widely throughout the Roman Empire. Jesus is a genuine dissident; he conveys the message that God belongs to everyone. He looks beyond the spiritual boundaries of his own community. He looks at the Romans: they conquer our bodies, we conquer their souls. We resist the empire spiritually.

Recognition of the hopelessness of armed partisan struggle was followed by the appearance of the strategy of nonviolent spiritual resistance. If a dominant empire occupies a small nation, violence and nonviolence are realistic political-strategic alternatives. How might we liberate ourselves?

Jesus was a moral guerrilla, a violator of censorship: they condemned him to death for the things he said. The Jewish defendant was convicted by a Roman judge, with collaboration from the Jewish priestly authorities. The people preferred to save the life of Barabbas, the partisan leader, who was a rogue like many partisans in our century. Rogues are always called terrorists by the other side.

Jesus's era was a wild time too, just like times in general. In the land of the Jews, Jewish teachers were killed by the thousands. According to the Chronicles, Jesus thought with magical passion, in public. He turned from the sword and accepted the cross. His crucifixion is not the image of resignation, however. In a few hundred years, the victim succeeds in conquering the Roman Empire.

77. Why couldn't the idea of total nonviolence win over Jesus's Jewish countrymen? Historical reality proves that later it didn't win over the Christians either, but that is no answer. The spirit of Jesus is one genuinely alien to every kind of territorial-ethnic xenophobia, Jewish and Christian included; it is a radically supra-national and planetary spirit.

The Christian denominations could not have existed, however, had they not blessed arms, had they not made pragmatic agreements with aggressive regimes of all eras. Historical Christianity was no less realistic than rabbinical Judaism.

As far as religious violence is concerned, the Crusades, the persecution of heretics, the religious wars, and the Inquisition were not initiated by rabbis.

78. If life is sacred, then life, the family, the city must be protected, said the Jews. If need be, the Jew is not a bad soldier. Jewish legionnaires were in demand in the Roman Empire.

It is also a fact that Jews are more excited than the average people by the relationship between ideal and reality. They find it difficult to accept contradiction between thought and practice.

They do not gladly profess ideas they will certainly not practice. Pragmatic and sanctimonious hypocrisy is not a typically Jewish attribute.

The armed guerrillas surely told Jesus's followers: We must not allow another nation to occupy our homes and give us orders. They might have the advantage in force now, so maybe armed struggle against the empire now would be foolish, but if there is a chance of victory, why shouldn't we fight? Why shouldn't we liberate ourselves completely from that which burdens us? We've had enough of being dominated! Enough crucifixions! Enough of the rule of Jewish eminencies who collaborate with the Romans! Jesus's contemporaries, combative young Jews, must have said these kinds of things to him.

Similar thoughts have always been said and will always be said by young, combative men. People say there is proportional retaliation. Long ago they might have said: If a nation wants to be free of its occupiers, who are completely unwilling to leave of their own accord, armed aggression is justified.

79. I should have not mother, father, wife, or child? I should have only a spiritual covenant with twelve other men who have also left their families? I should castrate myself for the land of paradise? Then how will I have children? Should a child not be conceived in rapture? What sort of teaching is this? How can I adhere to this?

Eschatological doctrines. But the Jews hold continuity of the family to be the highest value! Who doesn't? Don't Christians, don't Muslims?

Many Jews felt that the Christians deified a man no one would want to follow. A folk religion, the religion of community does not regard suffering or martyrdom as its highest, most sacred value. The ancient Jews must have sensed something rash in such a choice, a youthful gesture that could engender hypocrisy.

They needed a religion that gave guidance to the paterfamilias. Jews were not lacking in courage; they could die martyrs' deaths. But God sentenced the Jew, the offspring of Abraham, to survival as a family, to work and love, to celebration and meditation.

80. The majority of Jews did not believe that the Messiah had truly appeared, in the image of that particular young man. He preaches meekness, then overturns the tables of the pigeon sellers and the money changers? He threatens the stubborn with the tortures of hell, the stubborn being those who do not follow him, those who do not follow his teachings? This is familiar, all the prophets are hot-tempered and self-centered, enchanted with their own truth while they belittle the truth of others: they are poets, and the literate are always getting in their way.

But why would a prophet be God? That a certain person, born of a mother, should be God: this may well have seemed a pagan fairy tale. Near-Eastern folk mysticism. God is God, man is man, and the two cannot be one.

Jewish skepticism could not and did not wish to imagine a relationship more corporeal than dialogue between the divine and the human. It was too modest. In contrast to the gods of other peoples, the God of the Torah did not pass the night with earthly women.

Jews only had false messiahs, so many impostors. In the sharp eyes of the rabbis, everyone who claims to be the Messiah, or whom others claim is the Messiah, is very suspicious. The promise of a personal savior, it seems, must not be granted.

81. The more severely they were persecuted, the more stubbornly the Jews stuck to the idea of One God whose depiction in human or animal form is idolatry. That God should impregnate a human woman, take on the form of His own son, and then fly back to himself through the death of the son?

In the eyes of the Jews, this sounded like a popular fairy tale in the Greek style. They believed that human imagination was a priori not capable of conceiving of God. God is always more, always bigger, always different.

God is the religious formulation of the fact that an intelligence inconceivably greater than ours is at work in the world, and that the knowledge we possess today is a mere spark compared to all that can be known.

Do not pull God down to the level of your own image. Man is fatefully mired in the image of man, because his imagination is weak. It is very hard work to liberate God from the comfortably, sentimentally human.

82. Reading the story of the anthropomorphic mediators as a novel, it is striking how frail, vain, easily angered they are, especially when they assert that they are superhuman, or have arrived from another world, when they refer to their special connections, while their listeners give signs of doubting them.

There has not been a time in my life when I did not read the Bible. I read the whole of it, like a great novel written with folk and metaphysical realism.

Jesus's warning that there will be gnashing of teeth if he is not heeded, I would list alongside the other moral ambiguities in the book, Adam's betrayal, Moses's ravings.... They make it a good novel.

The figure of Moses doesn't make me uncomfortable; he is quite human. As one of us, he dreamt the most daring dream about us and made us the people of monotheism. There was never any doubt, however, that Moses belongs among us, among humans. The God of Moses doesn't conceal Himself in Chinese universalist fashion—in an old man, in a stone, in flowers. He is, instead, our permanent partner in life. Dreamers and prophets hear His voice in their consciences. And the Unnameable comes, warns, promises, appeases, wants something from everyone, personally.

83. The Unnameable doesn't give away much about Himself: I am that I am. This is the main attribute of God conceived in the Jewish mode, the axiom of identity.

Like God, a person or a nation should also be what he or it is. Jesus's recommendation—Be perfect like your father in heaven—is a reference to this idea. Radical advice.

The Jews were not afraid, they did not deify their fellow humans, they did not bow before the statue of the emperor. In the eyes of a Jew, God is a mysterious infinity; the finite biography of a man can reveal about God no more than a shard of mirror can reveal about the sun. Softening the border between the human and the divine offends the Jewish sense of propriety.

84. I accept the illumination of the greatest saints and wise men. I consider the illuminated to be credible researchers and teachers of the idea of God. This Buddhist notion was a likable one to me from the beginning. Jesus is a wise martyr, like Rabbi Akiba. He was illuminated, like Jeremiah or Franz Kafka. Confucius, Lao Tse, Zoroaster, and Muhammad are all entitled to be included in that company.

I tend to accept every wise person as a prophet. I do not force myself to regard him as a superhuman being. It is human ranking only that separates those who know from the ignorant. The prophet justifies himself only by the things he says. He is like a writer. If he speaks badly, they forget him. False prophets are bad writers.

From the mystical perspective, the criminal and the fool can also be accepted as carriers of divine meaning. The real knower is not the one familiar with the teaching but the one who questions it.

With a little theological pluralism, the separation of worldly and spiritual literature could have been avoided. It was not; the two literatures broke apart fatefully, perhaps more to the detriment of the spiritual one. The notion that history cannot be altered does not mean that it is unconditionally worthy of respect. The divine being the domain of theologians is something poets, as professional mystics, have never taken seriously.

A child, too, can receive inspiration from another dimension. We can have mysterious contacts with intelligence surpassing ours, blessed be the name of inspiration's source.

85. The hypothesis of God's existence cannot be weakened by scientific rationalism. The dogma of the divinity of Jesus of Nazareth, of his immaculate conception and his corporeal resurrection, is a much tougher test for our doubting reason. Here, there is a genuine need for the blind leap of faith.

My mind can accept and believe in the Almighty. I can believe in an intelligence I cannot fathom, one affecting the world. I can believe with my whole consciousness in a consciousness of the world that surpasses mine absolutely. But if I wanted to believe in the divinity of Jesus, I would be able to do so only by conscious effort.

The more Christology accommodates the spirit of modern man—in other words, the more personal Christ is, the closer he comes to the faithful, the more he is depicted as our brother rather than our king—the more convincing and likable the ethic becomes. But, Jesus's theological status is made even more parenthetical, to be viewed in a separate realm of our intelligence.

86. It is a fact that the image of God become man secured a path to victory for Jewish monotheism—with some modification. Not accepting success in terms of numbers as the chief measurement of truth is the habit of minorities and Jews.

Paradoxically, the same story of the son that helped the Jewish God reach the polytheistic Romans makes spiritual thought more difficult in today's Christian culture, and eases the spread of secularization.

Had Jesus's Jewish biographers not made too great a concession to the Roman Empire's folk polytheism in the age of the man-god Caesar, modern culture would not have built up the secular value system, and secular knowledge, in isolation from the spiritual worldview, and then there wouldn't be mute incomprehension today between Judaism and Christianity, or even between Christianity and Islam.

Those with power are not too concerned about spiritual values. Churches and religious spokesmen do not aim for spiritual dialogue; they favor orthodoxies and value borders more than transcendence within them.

87. Jews always say the Messiah will come someday. I believe there have been many here, we just haven't noticed them. People save themselves by doing their bit and by loving whom they are given to love.

Who can absolve me from the weight of my sins? I must carry this backpack as long as I live. Not even the hand of a priest can take it off my back.

Heaven and hell are one and the same; now and eternity are one and the same; to me these equations are Jewish ideas. I am responsible for my actions forever. A person should stand eye to eye with his own God. We can cover our eyes to shield them from His light, but we cannot hide behind the back of another man.

The human plane is our lifetime: quite a long night onstage. Our freedom, our drama is the activity to which we give our time, the role we play. You get nothing for free here; every choice has a price. Every choice made is equivalent to rejection of the paths not taken. Every flight of life is a plummeting toward death. Yes, the field of our lifetime is but a miserable prison cell. There is no consolation.

88. For Jews, learning and praying are operations of similar meaning. Study can be conceived as the opening up of time, the overcoming of death.

Let us live, but not at any price. Die rather than be a traitor, said my tired, bent-backed old religion teacher, who had many daughters and a very small income.

The maintenance of a relatively closed group is provocative in any case. The harder the fate of the Jews was, the more obstinately they clung to their image of God sanctifying life. They held on to the idea of being chosen. The thought that the Jews have special tasks took root in them.

We humans must, in any case, fulfill the conditions of the contract. A unilateral advance of trust. The covenant between God and man is the Law, the Word, which is more than man but less than the Almighty.

The rabbis cast doubt on God's fulfillment of the contract in the death camps. There were those who said: This should have been neither done nor allowed. God betrayed us.

A very devout person said: Our covenant with God is not for just one generation. Whether He breaks His word, and how He means His word, is His business. God's mistake does not justify ours.

Truly not, said a young rabbi; we should have been more prescient and courageous. It is not enough to lean over the sacred books. The great, saintly scholars were not able to tell the rest of the Jews which course to take. The wise were not wise enough.

89. With this unilateral and axiomatic insistence on the idea of the contract, we did well, from a certain point of view. Unilateral loyalty is not a bad strategy for self-preservation. It is paired with an industrious life and the nurturing of talents.

From another point of view, it is a bad strategy: wherever Jews showed facility, from finance to music, the others became all the more suspicious. We have paid for not being allowed to let ourselves go to seed. We worked, studied, achieved successes, but it is a fact that this did not make us loved in the Europe of the Christians.

Curiosity, suspicion, envy, some attraction, a desire to overcome and dominate. Who knows all that colors ancient and eternally new anti-Semitism, which is not weakened at all by Jewish merits and accomplishments.

90. The argument that Christians' uncertainty with regard to Jesus contributed to Christian anti-Semitism convinced me immediately. Jesus of Nazareth, the king of the Jews, must be worshiped as God? How should the devout Christian handle the fact that Jesus, the disciples, the apostles, the first Christians were all Jews? As much Jews as were the Sanhedrin and those who stood around the cross and mocked Jesus in the story. The easiest solution was to forget this fact completely, to make Jesus a Christian, and to burden the Jews not with the covenant but, rather, with the role of the unchosen, to make them elected villains, for thousands of years, with the charge of deicide being raised anew every year at Easter. To make possible the killing of the Jews— non-Aryans, according to the Nuremberg laws—the aura of deicide was needed.

1981–88

Hungarian-Jewish Accounting

91. There are approximately one hundred thousand Jews in Hungary, mainly in Budapest—not really a community, not really a nationality, not really an ethnic group. It can be asserted that they are a part of the Hungarian people, and the same can also be denied. It can be asserted that they are a part of the Jewish people, and the same can also be denied. It can be said that they are Hungarian Jews, just as it can be said that they are Jewish Hungarians.

These uncertainties all tend to make the word *Jew* fit its object and include in its meaning everyone with anything to do with Jewishness, those who have Jewish sensitivity, consciousness; those who suffer from the historical serial murder designed to reduce the Jews in number and influence; those who may submit strictly to universal principles themselves but cannot be unbiased when it comes to another Jew; those who pale and brace themselves against the wall when the newspaper informs them a war has begun between Israel and its Arab neighbors; those who are angry when a Jew does wrong, the way only relatives can be angry.

In other words, there are almost a hundred thousand Jews here, or perhaps more if I also include those with a half, quarter, or eighth of functioning Jewish sensitivity, those who give a start upon hearing the word *Jew*, those whose well-being would be served by being able to wear this attribute like motherhood or fatherhood, those who would gladly work to be able to live with themselves and their fellow humans in tranquillity.

92. But if we have touched on the subject of tranquillity, that is something I find most readily in Hungary, in country houses, when my eyes see the sorts of things they were accustomed to from the beginning. I feel the same way about Budapest, when I'm in the mood to walk home from somewhere in the evening.

I started looking at women in this landscape; I have been in love mostly with women who live here. Here, I learned the order of life during the week and on weekends.

In the meantime, I learned of the great migration of peoples and the settlement of Hungary, of the Tatar invasions and the ravages of the Turks, then of our prolonged suffering at the hands of the Germans and increasingly, after 1849, at the hands of the Russians as well.

I am proud as one ought to be of Hungarian talents scattered over the world, the mainly Jewish Nobel Prize winners from the Italian evangelical high school on the avenue, the almost two thousand American university professors, drawn largely from the emigration of 1956. I feel at home in the company of the generation of 1956, in the company of those who were young around 1956.

I feel Késmárk and Brassó are not far away. My father attended business school in Késmárk; my uncle was the manager of the Korona Hotel in Brassó.

On long-distance flights, if I discover that my neighbor is Hungarian, I speak to him or her through the whole flight or, if not for the duration of the flight, in any case much more than I would with another passenger. I am more curious about the circumstances, smaller and larger, of a Hungarian traveling companion's life; things connect us; we can speak about the country where I usually live, where I can communicate with my fellow humans in my native language, where I learned the taste of foods and the smell of gardens, where my senses took possession of the world.

And since, as a Jew, I am also the son of a people who traditionally live through words and pay attention to the verbal environment, how can this language, Hungarian, the language in which my consciousness is expressed, fail to fill me with sensual pleasure? How can I be indifferent to the language that is the body of my spirit, or indifferent to all those with whom I naturally speak this language?

As a son of the Jewish people, I am a citizen of Hungarian society, the Hungarian nation, the Hungarian state. The larger part of my life has been spent among Jewish and Christian Hungarians, so how could I not be Hungarian? Am I both, then? Yes, both. The two can be made one only by denying the truth of life.

93. My being born Jewish and Hungarian is a double calamity. Two instructively unfortunate peoples. The existence of a white Anglo-Saxon Protestant, for example, is undoubtedly less open to question than that of a Hungarian, a Jew, or a Hungarian Jew. The WASP smiles more confidently for a reason.

Long torn by misfortune (*Balsors, akit régen tép*, from the Hungarian national anthem), that's how the poet characterizes his people in the verse an entire nation sings with deep emotion on holidays. The history of the last century and a half has made the verse into the Hungarians' cult song. We sang the anthem not less than three times in a row on Madách square, in December 1956, to force the police to stand at attention, as they prepared to beat us with the flats of their swords from astride their horses and with rubber truncheons on the ground. One must remain still during the anthem. When we had bound ourselves together for a third time through this device, they did not strike, and we dispersed. Not a great triumph, I'll admit, but at least we didn't hurt each other.

Well, the Jews could say the same about themselves: long torn by misfortune. Fate rips, tears away at these two peoples. Both are fully aware of it and tend to grieve for themselves, to keep an inventory of their injuries and defeats, which they refuse to forget.

94. Two peoples of fourteen to fifteen million souls each. Both have a large diaspora. The nationhood of both was made doubtful or actually suspended for a long time. Both could feel and did feel threatened in their very existence as a nation-people-community. Many of both emigrated to America at the beginning of the century. A third of world Jewry and two-thirds of Hungarian Jewry were victims of violent death in World War II. At the same time, every twentieth Hungarian died in the war. Jews and Hungarians have many common experiences, they have lived through a lot together in the course of time.

It is a fact that nowhere in Europe was the numerical proportion of Jews to non-Jews higher than it was among Hungarians. Yet the Germans were more intolerant of their Jewish minority.

If there remains a significant Jewish community in Central Eastern Europe, this is it. The greater part of Hungarian Jewry was murdered, and many of the rest left, because they did not feel secure here. Many left because their existence was put into question time and time again. First as Hungarians, then as citizens, then possibly as intellectuals. They got fed up. How many times can a person be made questionable before he loses patience?

95. Do Hungarians want the remaining Jews to stay here? Now that the citizens of the country have begun to speak more openly,

discussion of the presence of Jews cannot be avoided. Individuals and communities are introduced to each other. The coexistence of Christian and Jewish Hungarians is the real cultural question underlying the "folk-urban" opposition.

Since Christian Hungarians have had unpleasant experiences in connection with a number of Jews over the past decades, and since those Jews were figures of authority, it is natural for the experiences to seek expression. It is not mandatory to progress from memory to paranoid generalization, but this psychological process makes its way along a well-trodden path. It tempts by seeming to hand over the key to your problems. Our problem isn't the system, said many in recent years, but rather the Jewish functionaries. The bad advisers to the good king.

In recent years, it became clear that it was the system after all and not just a few scheming figures. The pious imagination appears to need someone in a devil's mask; it is not satisfied by sociological abstractions. The pietistic imagination demands that the guilty be named. Now that freedom of speech is increasing, will the speech of a new anti-Semitism appear, and if it does, how fast will it spread? Will it appear only on the far right, and only in allusions even there, with an electoral influence under ten percent?

And which will the Christian Hungarian intelligentsia choose—a self-definition that is open or one that is clamped shut, one that learns or one that is regressive? Will it interpret the Hungarian nation as a territorial-political and cultural phenomenon or as an ethnic-racial and religious one? Will it again desire ethnic homogeneity?

96. If a public-opinion poll were to ask Christian Hungarians whether they wanted Hungarian Jews to stay on in Hungary or to leave and go elsewhere, and if the majority were to say that the Jews should go—to wherever they want, Israel, America, wher-

ever they are accepted, but away from here in any case, because the sight of them offends our eyes—then Jews' insisting on friendship would not be a wise move.

Sooner or later, Hungarians probably would be seized by the same feeling toward the remaining Germans and Gypsies. Then other minorities with awakening consciousness would come to offend the eyes of the majority in its excommunicating mood, and then the wish to protect the purity of the race would emerge again, and the population could shrink to quite a small size, since Hungarians who do not have ancestors of another ethnicity a few generations back are the minority rather than the majority in this country. In the thousand years the Hungarians have reigned here, the country has had plenty of traffic; it has been a place of settlement and burial for armies and wanderers. For example, Jews lived here before Hungarians, if we believe the tombstones of Aquincum with their Hebrew lettering. Jews most likely came from the east too, possibly together with the Magyar tribes. Jews came from the north, south, and west as well during the entire course of Hungarian history. Jews, just like Hungarians, wanted to take root, build a nest, establish a home. When they weren't being expelled, Jews noticed that they were able to make a living from their trades, that they got along with the Hungarians, that the two peoples had a thing or two to learn from each other.

97. The people of this land, when they were able to read, grew up on poems, stories, and sayings all written and collected into one volume by Jewish people and translated into Hungarian. The people of this land were more suited to the single God, to a God who is reluctant to be the God only of the Hungarians, who wears the face of destiny instead. Because who knows what tomorrow will bring and what fate will disclose; who knows the direction from which misfortune, in the form of armed men, will come to the marketplace?

Let God be with us. The God who ravaged the Jews monstrously too, or just allowed them to go up in flames. The God who even let infants perish in the gas chamber. The God who— if He has any kind of goodwill toward his chosen people—used it most enigmatically in World War II. One could say he concealed it.

Hungarians and Jews both ask for God's blessing, for a more joyful year after the persecuted one hid away, and a sword forced him into his cave (*Bújt az Üldözött, s' felé kard nyúl barlangjában*— from the Hungarian national anthem). Though it isn't a nice thing, those who have been hurt will probably hurt one another too. To ask for generosity from the unfortunate is no small request. We should make up or split up for good, the radical thinker would say, who doesn't know about the durability of bad marriages.

98. There is no mention of Jesus. The Hungarian also believes in a single God, if he has faith at all, according to my reading of Hungarian poetry. In Trans-Tiszania, where I was born, the crucifix is rare, but Jews there are used to those squat Trans-Danubian Jesuses on their stone crosses. After all, he was one of us, one of our prophets, one of the true.

What does Jesus say? You should love God and your fellow man. We try to. It isn't always easy. The prophets said the same thing. Wise men have always said it.

Jesus didn't say, "Worship me, for I am your God," only, "Come to the Lord." An unscrupulous Jewish agitator, Saul, who became Paul, was the one who said Jesus must be worshiped as God.

There is a kind of strictness, an unbelieving soberness in the eyes of peoples battered by fate. Being gullible again could cause their downfall. They know that one can say many things. When the Hungarian Christian and the Hungarian Jew pray to their Lord and God, they basically speak to the same entity. An unpredictable God of fate, who sometimes softens toward them and then is understanding itself. They pray to the father, though they haven't been pampered much.

A religious contract is more significant than a legal contract, because I fulfill my part of the religious contract even if the other party treats me poorly, even if I could say that the contract has been broken. I fulfill the contract, because the religious contract is something like our feelings toward parents, siblings, spouses, children, and friends: we love them even if they're bad. Because our gesture is offering a hand, giving an advance, giving for free.

There are some who extend credit to the Lord with the hopeless obstinacy of the lottery player who doesn't skip a single week though he never wins. If He denies it to me, maybe He will give it to my children. If not to them, then to my grandchildren. And if I have no grandchildren, maybe He will bestow it on that child there on sidewalk across the street.

If the God and prayer of Hungarians and Jews are similar, then the two peoples could look at each other like neighbors in a hospital ward. It is in their interest to give each other a glass of water.

99. We must also consider the possibility that the majority desires our departure. Due to various errors, the experiment in cohabitation might not work. A divorce never happens because of the error of one party only. We could all go to Israel; there is a country that accepts us, one in which we have the right to citizenship. Many of us could go to America or other countries. We could leave if we again felt hostility toward us spreading in Central Europe, satisfying who knows what kind of need. Hostility can be institutionalized gradually into ideology. If they again call us alien to the people, we must go where neither "alien to the people" nor "class alien" appears in the dictionary of government or leading public opinion.

They are mistaken, and the new purifiers' cleanliness does not differ much from that of purifiers in general, but that is another question. Our experience leads us to conclude that dignity is more important than geography. Responsibility toward our children would suggest that if the purifiers want us out, we should go. We will not repeat the old game, in which we were gradually squeezed out of existence, always "understanding" those doing the squeezing.

Just as the remaining Jews left Poland and Bulgaria, Romania and Czechoslovakia, and just as many leave and many more wish to leave the Soviet Union, we could lose our faith in the reasons we persevered here in Hungary, or more specifically in Budapest, which is, as far as I know, home to the largest Jewish community between Paris and Moscow. On the road to Moscow, we should not forget Kiev, however.

Should we all go across to the western, Christian, liberal, capitalist democracies, where our livelihoods and our thinking fit into the surroundings? Or should we make our way at last to the sacred city, in spite of the continuing Jewish-Arab conflict? Should we endeavor to gain a foothold in the land of our ancestors, fighting and negotiating with others who also regard the sacred city as the land of their ancestors? Should we Jews struggle with one another, should we lose our enthusiasm for mankind through vexation over our own kind, complaining of decadence and corruption in the land where the fundamental law gives us the unquestionable right to exist?

Should we declare that the story of the Jews in Eastern Europe is over? Should we say we are not able to take part wholeheartedly in the Christian-national enthusiasm of the peoples of Central and Eastern Europe? Those who give themselves over to such enthusiasm are willing to think nostalgically of pre-1945 Hungary, something for which the Hungarian Jew has no cause to think nostalgically.

100. Or if our brand of difference is unbearable to the majority, if we ourselves long for a less ambiguous identity, if we long for that identity to be located here, where we are, should we follow in the footsteps of the Jewish neo-Catholics or neo-Protestants of the 1930s? Should we convert and become offended if Christian Hungarians continue to regard us as Jews?

Dismissing the assimilation scheme of the international socialism of the 1950s and 1960s, should we experiment anew with the alternative of the national conservatism or populism of the 1920s and 1930s?

Should we obscure certain biographical facts? Should we try to appear different from what we are? Should I not say that my father and grandfather were Jewish hardware dealers in Berettyóújfalu? What should I say instead? That my great-grandfather and my great-great-grandfather were Jewish tavern keepers in Berettyószentmárton? Should I deny that my Cohenite ancestors—if the tradition holds true—were priests, centuries before the birth of Jesus, in the great Temple of Jerusalem? I bow my head to touch the remains of the Temple's walls the same way I do when I touch the wall of the synagogue in Berettyóújfalu, now the warehouse for the hardware store that has been fashioned from my childhood home. Should we leave, because all that's left here is a remnant, living its final hours?

Or, if we are so attached to this place, to being Hungarian, then why shouldn't we be completely absorbed, through mixed marriages, if need be, and why shouldn't we be grateful for being received? After all, Christian Hungarians are the host majority, while in the eyes of many we are just troubling sojourners.

Should we disappear through melting into the majority, through mimicry, losing our marks of distinction not just on the surface but deep down too, so the hosts need not be disturbed by any variance? Should we justify the anti-Jewishness of others by our own Jewish self-hatred? Should we complete the assimilation, so that we might be reborn as good Hungarians? Our exertions would be appreciated—with some reservations, of course: that's still not it, it's still not perfect, we are still not different enough from what we really are.

101. Many Jewish friends of mine left after November of 1956, because they believed only two extremes were possible in Hungarian politics: either Stalinist, post-Stalinist repression or the return of the right, which would open a path for spontaneous anti-Semitism. There wasn't time for their pessimism to be proved or disproved; each used his preexisting orientation to speculate on what would happen if the Russians didn't return. I said that something new would come about, and with the Russians it would go underground. That's why I stayed. They shrugged and said I was a dreamer. They said that what would come about would be similar to what had been, something they needed no more. They left, because they had had enough of communism too.

I believed a sane democracy could be fashioned here, one in which big-mouthed haters try to acquire an audience but do not have many faithful, because the majority of people place themselves near the sober center. In 1956, just as now, I sensed that people did not believe the demagogues, and I thought that right-wing extremism would be only a marginal phenomenon. My sense of reality whispered it to me.

Then we slogged through it, everyone in his own way, through the more restrained, more practically minded, post-Stalinist repression, the Kádár era. The opposition was the enemy, throughout. A sort of devil, like the Jew in the mythology of anti-Semitism. After 1956, I didn't think the system had much strength left, I didn't think it could succeed in postponing public debate on fundamental and immediate questions for thirty-three more years.

102. Today still, there are observers both here and abroad, not only Jews, who fear that the democratic center in Hungary is only a weak transition to one of the extremes, to extremism of the right or left. They believe that liberal democracy is not the alternative to communism here, because liberal democracy is largely without precedents. The alternative is the nationalist feudal state, in which the spirit of the Horthy era is reborn and modernized. It is hard to forget that that spirit undertook the role of German satellite state; out of geostrategic Realpolitik considerations and, more or less, out of gratitude for the returned territories, it enacted the Jewish laws. Then—also by legislative means—it packed three-quarters of Hungarian Jewry onto trains and handed them over to the Germans, with a fair idea of the fate awaiting them beyond the border.

103. In my judgment, this queasy anticipation of the renaissance of the reactionary mentality was exaggerated at the end of 1956, and could only refer to sporadic events. But someone who has lived through a deportation has an idea of the outrageous deeds many good people are capable of if the outrageous deeds remain unpunished, if they are actually prescribed by a higher command.

Friends returning from Anglo-Saxon universities remind me that a long education necessarily precedes the achievement of civilized moderation and self-discipline, which protects against hysteria and knows that hysteria does not excuse crime. Friends who left the country out of such considerations are not sure if the civil moderation essential to democracy has ripened here in the meanwhile. They are also uncertain whether the spirit of objectivity and dignity with regard to others has spread enough so that a person, a citizen, cannot be harmed, disadvantaged, or have his life threatened for belonging to any minority by nature. My friends have in mind the history of Hungary after World War II, when a person could be discriminated against, if not for being a Jew then for being born a bourgeois, for seeing no reason to turn against the basic norms of bourgeois behavior.

In a sane country, you cannot be harmed because of your religion, societal origin, or worldview. It is shameful to be an anti-Semite in a liberal democracy, because antipathy turning into ideology regarding any group is opposed to the whole of the democratic system, because discrimination against a minority does not conform to the spirit or ruling logic of democratic law.

104. Among Jews, many erred in choosing communist socialism rather than liberal democracy as their canon, because communist socialism did not give them security. It cannot be stated that the Jewish middle class stood up for civil liberty and the dignity of the individual more stalwartly than the Christian middle class did in recent decades.

Compared to their actual statistical numbers in Budapest, Jews were overrepresented in both the regime's cultural apparatus and in the democratic opposition. Incidentally, Jews are overrepresented in quite a few other groups, both in Hungary and abroad. They have turned up in so many intersecting trends that it takes an exceedingly nimble anti-Semite to tie it all into a succinct generalization.

In the Kádár era—the history of the slow loosening of a restored dictatorship—in this Communist court, many feathered their nests using bourgeois pliancy. Even today one is not quite certain of the enthusiasm of many for civil liberties.

Within the intelligentsia, almost to the present day, it has not been evident that individual dignity is the highest of all values. In this region, reigning institutional modes of thought had to operate sometimes with concepts of nation and sometimes with concepts of class. European humanism and the spirit of liberal democracy consistent with humanism, placing the liberty and dignity of the individual highest on the scale of values, were minority trends before the war and even afterward.

105. Jews are consistent with themselves only if they conform to the principles of liberal democracy. Based on our experiences up to this point, only liberal public conditions have made Jewish lives secure, Jewish existence fruitful and free of fear. Formal democracy more or less suits our intellectual and moral bent. The Torah, the tradition, and the lessons of Jewish history are all reason for us to stand by the axiom of equality of rights among individuals. Only if our equality is ensured can we be truly different, person by person. Jews need liberal democracy because communism is unstable and unpredictable. Communism may purify itself of the Jews who took part in such great numbers at the start, and take them to camps. The Jews who joined the apparatus of Stalinist power were dupes. Stalinism would have been built up without them, but since they volunteered, it used them as zealous instruments. This group was not culled from the prime of Jewry; the finer ones got out of the Party religion early on, or, more likely, they did not get mixed up in it in the first place. Communism chosen for its antifascism can later deport its antifascist adherents. Contemporary Jews did not know much about communism. They were not able to deduce that if the institution of deportation, or the institution of forcibly resettling individuals or even entire peoples, was consistent with the ruling ideology, then Jews were in danger, sometimes for one, sometimes for another of their qualities. The Jew is safe only in a society where no one may be deported, where the free citizen is the norm. If the free citizen is not possible, then the Jew is especially endangered.

106. The small must be careful most of all not to be petty or small-minded. A small people can behave generously. The role of

satellite is a nightmare for a small people, because it is tempting and dangerous. Tempting because it does indicate a realistic appraisal of relative power, and also because it converts the weaker party's situation, that of a loyal vassal to the liege lord, into advantages. Dangerous because the role can become a habit, even a reflex, something that can be called part of one's character. The years 1967 and 1968 were the zenith of the Kádár era, the initiation of the economic reforms. We began to believe we were pulling ourselves out. Breaking off diplomatic relations with Israel and invading Czechoslovakia together with the Soviets were not generous gestures. We accommodated too much, adapted too much, adjusted too well to being in the superpower's sphere of influence; we made the pattern mistake of small nations, behavior that suggests neither the master nor the serf but, rather, something between the two, perhaps an overseer who is not elected but appointed to give orders. His loyalty is toward his superiors rather than toward the people under him. The local leadership behaved with exaggerated conformity toward the Germans and then toward the Russians. In both cases, the leadership even hoped for territorial reparations in exchange for the tail wagging. Jews with roles in government participated substantially in this strategy. The national consensus on reform rather than revolution began to ripen, and the Hungarian elite, Christian and Jewish alike, was silent, myself included. My respect goes to the exceptions, whose names do not make a long list. We were therefore accessories to the government in these two unjustifiable acts. As I remember, we underestimated the historical symbolism of these two mistakes at the time. We know that collective moral missteps are not smoothed out in time; rather, they become increasingly distressing the more we know about them, because they reveal a latent national strategy that has brought and still brings only trouble. This clever little strategy is attracted to short-term advantages, commits hypocrisy and crimes to get them, and leads to unrealistic policy, defeat, and backwardness in every case. Over the long term, the clever little strategy is like going into debt. It is difficult to earn national moral-cultural capital, and easy to lose it. It is possible to go into debt morally as well as financially.

107. By unilaterally cutting off diplomatic relations with Israel, the official sphere of the Kádár regime betrayed Hungarian Jews at home, abroad, and those living in Israel. With the invasion of Czechoslovakia in August of 1968, we reprised the moral gesture of the 1940 invasion of Yugoslavia. In the role of satellite, our troops invaded a neighboring country with which we had signed friendship and nonaggression treaties earlier.

The lack of noteworthy internal resistance to these two betrayals shows how little sovereignty Hungarian civil society had at the time.

For some, the indifference may have been colored by anti-Semitism; for others, by irredentism. At the time, there was also the neonationalist view that the Russians might reinstate the Vienna decisions if we were loyal enough to them.

This foxy, small-nation survival strategy justifying every moral error and lie was the thinking that held the whole of the Kádár regime together. The acceptance of the lesser evil, the reconciliation with reality instead of with progress—"muddling through any way we can"—corresponded to the opinion of the decisive majority in Hungarian society of the era.

The Kádár regime needn't have executed so many people. There was no hanging after the repression of democratic experiments in Prague and Warsaw.

108. The Hungarian Jewish community was distressed by the Kádár government's official participation in eastern bloc anti-Zionist propaganda, which sometimes amounted to barely disguised anti-Semitism. One unpleasant memory is Jewish journalists' tak-

ing part in this anti-Zionist propaganda campaign, willingly formulating biased, pro-Arab, anti-Israel commentaries.

And let us remember the political and financial support (arms and training camps) the Hungarian government gave to military action against Israel. Our government censored Egypt, which made peace, and celebrated the Arab hard-liners, who made annihilation of the state of Israel a primary goal in their official documents. Until Arafat, in his own name, recently rescinded the article of the Palestinian Charter calling for the removal of the Zionist entity from the Middle East (which still doesn't mean that the position of the entire Palestinian leadership has changed), Hungarian foreign policy did not once raise its voice against the charter. It was an uncritical ally of the PLO; official policy regretted, at most, that the various factions of El Fatah were killing one another instead of turning all their strength against the common enemy.

The teaching or promulgation of the idea of Zionism was a political offense, cause for action by the political police. It was not good form to say a person was a Jew; there were repulsive euphemisms instead: "those persecuted by Nazism," or, if absolutely necessary, "of Jewish origin." As if Jewish origin were something that could be tolerated but being a Jew consciously, as an adult, was not quite proper.

The regime encouraged participation in the ostensible public consensus: one could become a part of the collaborating elite of the Kádár era, vocal or silent as prudence dictated; one could accept the prizes, the favors, but one had to keep quiet about the difficult matters and know the limits exactly. Jewish writers didn't identify themselves as Jews. They restyled themselves not as members of the working class but, rather, as part of the Christian middle class.

109. Among younger Jewish women and men, those born after the war, many did not know that they were Jews, or, if they were

told, the revelation was accompanied by the parental commentary that it didn't matter. Later these youths made friends with other similar youths, to whom it also didn't matter.

Together and with great difficulty, they noticed that directness in addressing God and critical-ironic distance, this quite Jewish paradox, was something close to them, and not just because the play of intimacy and distance was an essential creative element of modern European cultural development.

One should consider the works of Jewish authors in which the word *Jew* does not even appear, still readable in their entirety as reflections on Jewish identity. As it journeys toward the end of the millennium, why can't a generation that smashes through censorship put its diverging identities in front of the same carriage?

110. A new situation has emerged. Probably the one we were waiting for. For myself, I can say that this is what I wanted: the hour of truth, when everything is spoken, in turn. When unctuous dishonesty is not the prerequisite of survival.

Will there be democracy here, if there hasn't been up to now? I believe there will be. Every democracy had to start somewhere. Yes, I believe we will transform ourselves into a democratic state of law. With the decay of censorship, my impression is that a stylistic turn is also taking place. Suddenly, not calling things by their names, sweeping things under the carpet, making things "not happened" by not speaking of them, laughing things off— all begin to appear unnatural and embarrassing.

Christians and Jews alike tend to delude themselves that they are only naive victims who suffer events—never initiating, only reacting, and thus they are excused from any moral responsibility. In the depth of our souls, however, we all sense that the burden of responsibility is borne by an entire community, by everyone who learns the behavior and conditioning of his own people or society.

Both the Hungarians and the Jews tend to make attempts to liberate themselves, but it is a fact that both were deprived of sovereign statehood for a long time, and thus both tried to survive hard times in the role of the subordinated.

III. A young man voiced anti-Semitic epithets, and when he was called to question for it, he said: "If there is democracy, then anti-Semitism is allowed too. Isn't it?" And up to a point, that of inciting violence against Jews, he is basically right. Until now, neither the one nor the other was possible, neither a respected separate identity nor a rejection of the Jews.

Those who are more anxious fear societal explosions, because at such times it is easy to get hold of weapons on the street, a situation many Jews do not wish for. Who knows who will bang on the front door and why?

In Western Europe, Jews do not feel insecure, but to the east of the Rhine they do. German and Austrian desecrations in Jewish cemeteries, the expulsion of the remaining Jews from Poland twenty years ago, the anti-Semitism of today's Russian neofascists, after Stalin's, all are signs that anti-Semitism has remained virulent in Europe's eastern regions, even after World War II, even in the region conscientiously calling itself Central Europe.

112. Hungarian Jews are right to stay here if Hungarian constitutional democracy is viable. If the democratic transition and European integration have no chance, then the Hungarian Jew also has no chance here in the country of the Danube and Tisza. Then—out of responsibility to our children—we should abandon this remaining outpost. In democracies there is no political anti-Semitism, even if there is folk anti-Semitism.

How will Hungarian democracy fare? Will it move in the direction of goodwill and love of justice? Or are there still emotional and ideological grounds for anti-Semitism to appear as a political trend? We have to ask ourselves new questions.

If there are signs of political anti-Semitism reappearing in our environment, if, in other words, there is a repetition of that which separated the Hungarian political elite from the political elite of Western European democracies in the period between the two world wars, then a significant portion, possibly the most capable, of the remaining Hungarian Jews will say goodbye to Hungary. Then they will take their families to a place where they will not be subject to prejudice based on hysterical reactions to their nature as minorities. I call hysterical the anti-Semite who sees the hand of the Jews in every problem.

Hungarian Jews will feel at home in Hungary, here, where they were born, to the extent that they have the opportunity to live in a free country, to the extent they can agree with responsible Christian Hungarian fellow countrymen on the philosophy and morality of constitutional democracy.

If people belonging to various parties consider the morality and style of fair play compulsory and self-evident, then we will be able to walk on the street and feel we are at home.

113. Will it be a generally accepted truth that the cooperation of the one-time authorities in the annihilation of the majority of Hungarian Jews, six hundred thousand people, was a crime? Can a particular person honestly, credibly accept collective responsibility?

When I accept being part of a community, I prefer to accept a share in its glory. But if I accept its tradition of virtue, am I not obliged also to accept a share in its tradition of sin? After all, virtue is always born of the struggle with sin and is never pure. A German cannot accept only Goethe and Beethoven from the German past; a Russian cannot choose only Pushkin and Chekhov. Accepting also means wanting to remember, and suffering. We get the entire past of our chosen community, a past that includes all its monstrous figures.

What do I accept as mine, if I was born into two communities? Sometimes the baggage of history weighs down on us. As Jews, we cannot think of ourselves as victims only, all the more because history preserves numerous accounts of Jewish deeds and doers. There is no people without sin, only moral insensitivity. We cannot refuse to accept Rákosi and his Jewish entourage as a weight on our souls. A Jew must suffer if Israeli soldiers shoot down Arab children.

114. Christian and Jewish Hungarians—two strong identities. One views things only from the Hungarian perspective; the other cannot forget being a Jew. The Jew cannot melt in like the German or the Slovak. It is impossible for the Jew not to have a dual identity. It is impossible for him not to feel a certain amount of solidarity with Jews living all over the world.

The Jew is able to imagine the path leading from aggressive speech to slaughter. The Hungarian cannot forget the horrific vision of the death of the nation. Two easily offended, thorny constitutions prone to a dark view of things. They remember an assortment of defeats, days of mourning and executions. The destruction of the city, the occupation of the country, the burning of loved ones, gassed parents, wives, and children; none of it can be forgotten.

In this region, only defeat creates community; we write much verse in the memory of death, our tombstones are more fantastic, our cemeteries more intimate than Western cemeteries. Can we at least extend a hand toward each other over the dead? If we were not able to keep them, let us at least keep their memories.

The Jew is the more judgmental, mercurial, radical, but intellectual rashness can bring about great foolishness. In the two real Hungarian revolutions, 1848 and 1956, the two communities met, and a part of them worked together. In an optimistic mood, we could say: it is a strange, attraction-repulsion relationship. As if the two peoples were complementary.

The relationship of Christian and Jewish Hungarians is one of the most interesting questions in Hungarian intellectual culture. The relationship now has another chance to clear up or become knotted. First there is curiosity, approach, preparation for friendship; then suddenly a kind of offended buttoning up, an injustice stored away and brought up again and again. Two peoples with scarred consciousness; they would like to view their past with more pride, but it isn't easy. In any case, the way I see it, in this freshest and intellectually most interesting revolution, the one now taking place within us and around us, we are again doing it together.

115. Every antidemocratic variant of anti-communism, every impetus toward the right driven by revenge, is contrary to the long-term interests of Hungarian Jewry. If the most significant portion of the Hungarian middle class decides against liberal democracy for some reason, the only alternative would be a marginal blend of nationalism and communism, a kind of national-Communist authoritarian state, with its own peculiar brand of paternalism.

The logical antithesis of liberal democracy is some sort of discriminative national-communist authoritarian system that impedes the Hungarian nation from being integrated into Europe.

Democratic world public opinion wants democracy in Hungary, as elsewhere, and such a goal is in the country's long-term interest in every respect. It's as if a door now opens before the Hungarian nation, and before the Jewish minority that is part of it, a chance to take a proper step in the direction of Western rationality.

In this affair, Hungarian Jews are every bit as involved as Hungarian Christians. It is now in the interests of quite a lot of forces that there be democratic political culture in Hungary, because it is the only one that makes possible a coherent value system and the emergence of the individual.

116. There were and are democrats in this country, both among Christian and Jewish Hungarians, but they were never in the majority. The majority tried to make it through the continuously hard times by collaborating to a greater or lesser degree. And there has also been a minority committed to a brand of political thought that emphatically denies the values of liberal democracy. Two fiascos accompanied these two extremisms. The swing to the right resulted in defeat in World War II, the renewal of Trianon, and a damaged national consciousness. Left-wing extremism brought another forty years of fear, strandedness, and dilapidation.

Democratic transformation is in the societal and national interest of Christian and Jewish Hungarians. There is no personal liberty, legal security, and civilized contact between citizens without constitutional democracy. According to all signs, it is also the condition necessary for the internal stability of nations and systems. In countries neighboring Hungary, only constitutional democracy provides personal and communal autonomy, as well as free contact with Hungarians of the mother country for the Hungarian minorities. The speeding up of democratization in the Central European region is in the national-societal interest of Hungarians. Hungary seems suitable for the role of active mediator, initiator, catalyst.

117. Jews all over the world have an interest in the building of constitutional democracy and adherence to the universal declaration of human rights. If Jews carry on practices contrary to this, then they act in contradiction to the historical interests of Jewry.

Jews in Israel are also faced by a fundamental option, the crossroads between nationalist and democratic priorities. Which do they choose: the occupied territories or democracy? If they keep the occupied territories, they cannot retain the spirit of democracy; they will be compelled to violate the human rights of the Arabs continuously. Then Israeli society will become militarized beyond the critical limit. As a reaction to isolation, resentment will reign, and the creative imagination will be stifled.

The nationalist-authoritarian option is automatically accompanied by censorship. Being in opposition to world public opinion and Israel's American supporters must be justified ideologically, permitted internally. If the Israeli political class places the expansive strategy of national defense above democracy for too long, Jewish consciousness in the world will find itself in a difficult situation.

118. The prime gesture of assimilation: uncritical acceptance of local values. Loyal accommodation to the reigning prejudices of national common knowledge—this was the error of traditional assimilation. This led to the anti-Semitic assessment: "No! It's not true that you are one of us!" False identification—on the part of Christians and Jews—was a demand that was accepted. "Be entirely Hungarian," said the freethinking integrators. "We are entirely Hungarian," panted the freshly integrated. The former asked for falseness, and got falseness. The latter promised falseness, and gave falseness. Good faith was there on both sides. But the substance of the agreement could only be a fiction.

This arrangement repeats itself up to the present day, and it makes one wonder. There are Christian Hungarians who demand complete assimilation on the part of Jews, and there are Jewish Hungarians who wish to eradicate the Jewishness in themselves, promising complete assimilation to the Christians. In the world of literature, too, there is demand and willingness to renew the false pact.

119. Let us make our values clear. The issue is the moral antin-omy of self-acceptance and self-denial. Self-denial can be thought of as a weaker version of self-negation. Self-denial is more like not facing one's self, like mistaken self-knowledge, mistaken po-litical self-definition, unstatedness, avoidance, purposefully mak-ing oneself and others forget.

The Jew who promises complete assimilation lies. He will not be able to keep the promise. Even if he commits aggression upon himself, if he falls into the error of Jewish anti-Semitism, Jewish self-hatred, which is accompanied by having to deny all solidar-ity with the local Jewish community and world Jewry, even so he will still never be able to forget the Jewish point of view on things.

The promise of assimilation contains the adaptation to anti-Semitism. On the Christian side, the demand for assimilation is a continuation of the Christian anti-Semitism of the Middle Ages, which demanded from Jews self-negation and conversion.

The demand for *assimilation* into the national culture is, as ever, the demand for apostasy or, perhaps more accurately, con-version. This time, conversion is used in a national-secular for-mulation, conversion to the nation as a folk-ethnic concept. This is impossible. To wish it or promise it is senseless.

On the other hand, the *integration* of the Hungarian Jewish community into the Hungarian nation is possible, into the nation as a linguistic, cultural, political, and territorial community, into the self-consciousness of those who hold a constitutional demo-cratic value system.

Of course, it is also possible for Hungarian Christians and Jews to come to terms with each other by mutually restyling them-selves as victims not bearing responsibility, extending the era of nonresponsibility over the entire Communist period, up to the present day. As moral newborns, their essence would be transformed if they both squinted hard enough.

120. In any case, we must be two, and we must distinguish ourselves from each other in order to reach an honest agreement. A bridge is only possible between two sides. We have lived together for a long time; we are identical and not identical. We could actually find something interesting in that.

Surely, we continue this tense cohabitation because beyond every disappointment we still find value, intimacy, or even erotic attraction in each other. We find a lot of things; durable relationships are unimaginable otherwise.

Much remains unsaid, and it is not even necessary to say everything. But it is time to speak now, time for us to formulate our agreements and our differences at least into an imaginary contract. Our honesty will cause only pleasant surprises, because if we declare ourselves identical at the outset, our differences will pop up unceasingly. If, however, we state at the outset that we are different, the common will be discovered time and time again.

121. There is a country where the Jews can go if everything falls apart. There is a piece of land where they can immediately become citizens with full rights. The country has been realized, it has institutions, politicians, conflicts. It is human and frail, in many respects resembling the countries of other peoples. But self-censorship and especially Jewish self-censorship ends there. Every Israeli citizen can behave as a conscious member of the Israeli nation, no matter where he is on the wide political spectrum. Life is not at all easy there, but one no longer has to contend with the question of disguising oneself as a matter of prudence.

122. But there was a hitch with Israel. The country was inhabited. Not very densely, but increasingly so. Liberated from Christian anti-Semitism, the European Jew finds himself smack in the middle of mainly Semitic Arab-Islamic anti-Judaism or, rather, anti-Zionism; he is squeezed into one nation with the eastern Jews in an increasingly Middle Eastern country, where Jews are faced with themselves. They are faced with the situation that has developed and exists. They must face what they do rather than the acts attributed to their phantom image.

123. If I accept Jewish identity, why am I not a Zionist? I espouse Zionism as a Diaspora Jew who might move to Jerusalem, among other places, for a time, but will spend the majority of his time in Budapest, speaking Hungarian.

I believe that there is a such a thing as modern Jewish culture, in various languages, to be found in various national cultures. It is not in the Hebrew or Yiddish language, and it is secular rather than religious. There is an international Jewish culture connected to the Jewish tradition only by spiritual threads.

The oft mentioned works of Jewish writers, thinkers, scientists can be analyzed also as reflections on identity, responses to Jewishness as a challenge, stylized self-portraits.

After Auschwitz only shock and stupor made us forget we were Jews. If you know the essence, you can bypass the ritual.

If you accept yourself as different, then you accept the others as different also. Then you recognize the sanctity of individual mediation. You can accept the Christian, the Hungarian, the Central European, and the inhabitant of the world in and around you only if you accept the Jew in yourself.

I have mentioned only one combination here; an infinite number exist. The person born a Jew should remain one but understand the other religions. Understanding is a more credible encounter than conversion.

124. Does a French, Polish, Russian, or Hungarian Jew consider himself more Jewish or more French, Polish, Russian, or Hungarian, or something completely different? Let the answer to this question depend on the person in question and not on someone else. Most likely, the internal balance will swing differently at different periods in a person's life.

Everyone is what he feels he is. I am no man's judge, to decide if he is Albanian enough or Belgian enough. I'm better able to determine whether he is wise or foolish.

I'm not very interested in others' judgment on whether I am Hungarian enough or Jewish enough.

As I see it, there is still a nonassimilating Jewish mentality—but not orthodox, not isolationist, and not Zionist—outside of Israel, in many countries.

I am Hungarian and I am Jewish, that's the way things have developed. It doesn't cross my mind to think one part is genuine and the other is not. I do not wish to dissect myself, nor could I.

Viewed from the Far East, I am probably Judeo-Christian. Hungarian, Jewish, European? I am typing these lines in Colorado Springs in August 1988. I spent the early summer vacation in Budapest; it's livelier there, more peaceful here. All four of my children are here; work is coming along fine, thanks.

I don't mind that I'm reading the daily newspaper *Magyar Nemzet* here. Up to now, my impression was that the majority of people live entirely inside their own cultures, accompanied by their local stereotypes. But the process of thinking cannot do without periodical distancing from our original environment.

125. Among radicals I was moderate; among moderates, radical; among Hungarians, a citizen of the world; in the world at large, Hungarian; among the bourgeois, marginal; among the marginal, bourgeois.

My purpose was not to antagonize the others but to protect something that I am, in addition to what makes me one with them.

I consider it my moral task to protect that larger domain left out of every consciousness of community, even the consciousness of love.

Before 1948, while there were still political parties in Hungary, I found something sensible in all their platforms. Among left-wingers, I find questions raised by the right ever more justified; among right-wingers, I feel the reverse.

Combative communal consciousnesses exile a significant part of human reality. Where there is exile, I am with the exiled. A writer may allow himself to take such a position, a politician may not. The politician must either create or pretend to hold the majority position.

As soon as the discourse turns political, the consensus of the ruling moral majority as a measure of things appears in the speaker's spiritual eye. He must know how far he may stray from it. Political speech must not only refer to the plural *we,* it must also take exception to the "bad" minority. These bad ones can be radicals or conservatives. If there is a *we,* then there must be a *they* as well, at whom we look askance. We exclude them from somewhere.

A multitude, not individuals, en bloc. If nothing else, we exclude them from moral respectability.

126. I identify the superiority in people with the indeterminate. He's a man? Why isn't he a woman? Adult? Why not a child? White-skinned? Why not colored? European? Why not Oceanian? A Jew? Why not a Buddhist? A writer? Why not a cook? That I am what I am is neither shameful nor glorious. The oak tree cannot be a beech tree. Should it brag of not being a beech?

127 It feels good to discover that understanding others is possible even when they are very different from us. A lover whose language I barely understand, an ancient Chinese philosopher, an Australian longshoreman's handshake in a bar on the coast, the

smile of a black saxophone player in San Francisco. The best in us is that which breaks through us and reaches the other person. Verbal and nonverbal understanding, crossing borders.

128. Most of my communication is directed at few people, possibly just one. Did you sleep well? Does it taste good? When are you coming home? Should I want my thinking to belong only to my circle of friends, to my family? Should I remain a strictly Budapest mind? I am quite enough so as it is. I'm always pulling out my stories of Budapest, in other cities too.

Even if I wanted to, I couldn't jump over my shadow. I take my kinsfolk, my neighbors even, on the most adventurous forays. The stone that has been heaved skyward should be proud of how high it flies and not proud of falling back down.

1989

On Jewish-Christian Reconciliation

129. The Bible is the literature of a God-creating people, written by many authors. Great individuals invite the listener or reader to go with them, they preach to the multitudes, and once they are alone, they all carry on a dialogue with the one and only God, but none of them are identical to Him. They are all different, all fallible, like writers in general. We read narratives by authors about exceptional figures and experiences.

Jewish and Christian fundamentalism, both considering religion an inviolable tradition, are allies inasmuch as they mutually reinforce the impossibility of dialogue between them, and to this extent they are relatives of Islamic and even communist fundamentalism.

If these two religions want to live, they must take account of the two thousand years that have passed since biblical times, of everything people have done and written since then. Both must take account of a third spiritual authority, world literature in the broad sense, within which the notion of centralist hierarchy is unthinkable.

In biblical, Talmudic, and rabbinical times, Jewish pluralism always existed, and it does now, if we read the texts of Jewish authors of the past two centuries. Christian pluralism also emerged, though not without a great struggle. Since the age of the Enlightenment, more or less tolerant coexistence has developed among Christian religions. Certainly the most important trend in political Christianity, Christian Democracy, considers pluralism a value it must hold and practice.

The older and the newer brother hold hands and look around on the planet, and perceive that there are more and more others around them, who believe or do not believe in their own faiths, just like Judeo-Christians. Only one quarter of humanity lives in the Judeo-Christian tradition; the time of global, all-encompassing religious dialogue is here. Conversation does not require conversion; everyone stays himself, with a better understanding of the other.

130. The relationship between man and God is always a drama. The human being searches for protection by something higher, and in hours of certainty he believes he has found it, but then other kinds of hours come, when the separation of God from existence does not appear to be necessary.

The Jew does not elevate above himself a God-become-man or a man-become-God; he takes account of the notion that the teachers believe they hear the word of God. He listens to them, but puts the holiday, the sanctification of family life, on the highest plane.

For some, God is in their existence, in their every act, and therefore they do not wish to speak of Him separately. Do they speak to God or to their own consciences? They beg, "Don't leave me." Embittered, they say, "Why did you leave me?" The relationship between God and man is made dramatic by our mortality; it is a personal affair and an intimate one; it doesn't really have much to do with those who invoke His name in vain, as if He were an instrument of their profession.

131. Now that the state culture of socialism has collapsed, many search for a simplified paradigm and a simple opposition. Some of those who discovered the Christian in themselves just recently will readily make the occasional anti-Semitic remark before long. The newest trend is for religious authority to take the place of state authority, and the uncertain person covers himself with the language of religion. From the church to the party, from the party to the church.

I am suspicious of those who suddenly trade in their socialist phraseology for religious phraseology. Following intolerant state-culture, they return to religious intolerance.

There is a one-book, fundamentalist type of personality that is respectful of authority and wishes to demean competitors religiously and piously at once. Yesterday, Tartuffe was a Marxist-Leninist. How about today?

132. In the eyes of clear-sighted Jews and Christians, salvation is not yet completed. The calamities have not yet past; we are not yet free from human evil. In this light, every good act is a crumb of salvation. Salvation? Absolution. Conciliation. Reconciliation. Settling down. Eternal dream. Liberation from the sufferings inherent to our nature as humans. "Death was his salvation."

133. Incinerating people necessitates the existence of institutions that are on good spiritual terms with murder but obfuscate that relationship with confusing speech.

There will always be friction and jealousy between the younger and the older brother. Reconciliation means learning from each other. But from which position? Not from two spiritual foxholes; since we are not completely and only Christians or Jews, we must learn instead from our existence in the here and now.

Here we stand, Christian and Jewish Hungarians, Europeans who have become more or less worldly, not very religious for the most part, and we cannot think of anything more intelligent than human individuals having equal political rights and equal ethical-metaphysical rank. The fundamental idea of human rights more or less reconciles Christians and Jews with each other, as well as with all other peoples.

134. To describe a person, many more words are needed than *Jew* or *Christian*. We need to be wary once more of the abstract and high-flown. The possibility of a dishonest turn is again here: after a quasi-religious stance on the left, we may take a quasi-religious stance on the right. After compulsory atheism, compulsory religion. Both violate freedom of conscience. The admixture of religion and politics results in nothing good. If we do not separate these two human dimensions, we will once more confuse political concepts and give up precise speech.

Dialogue unclamps; the challenge for the two parties is to re-live and personally create the spirit of their religion within themselves. A human being must not submit his freedom of conscience to any human institution, neither state nor church. European experience has proved that the dignity of the human individual is an unvanquishable value.

1990

Marginal Notes
to the Ten Commandments

135. Jews, Christians, Muslims—almost half of humanity—hold sacred the ten moral commandments that God conveyed to the people, as it is written, using his spokesman Moses. Between God and the people the Ten Commandments are the content and price of the covenant.

These ten commandments mean something to the people; they disturb the people if contravened; they compel guilt and contrition, stimulate hypocrisy, and they do not let go. They wound people's innocence.

A moral being is one who knows right from wrong, and then acts either rightly or wrongly. As soon as people accepted the Ten Commandments as a set of unconditional rules, they accepted the notion of sin, and the notion of wavering between ignorance and the call of God. Their actions are simultaneously decisions bearing personal responsibility to the unnameable authority.

136. Honor your parents. Do not kill, steal, bear false witness, or covet that which belongs to your neighbor. In other words, do not do unto others that which you do not wish done unto you. Thus

commanded the voice to the people, who were on occasion dishonorable toward their parents, who killed, stole, bore false witness, committed adultery, and coveted that which belonged to their neighbors. But the word was branded into the memory of the people.

...and they took their stand at the foot of the mountain...
And Mount Sinai was wrapped in smoke, because the Lord descended upon it in fire; and the smoke of it went up like the smoke of a kiln, and the whole mountain quaked greatly...

And those that stood there heard: "I am the Lord, your God."
Infinite power addresses us; God comes to the person, but stays invisible and does not want to be seen. If He could be seen, then He could be depicted, and with images to deify we might be able to make easier bargains with the absolute commandments and prohibitions.

No middle road is offered between killing and not killing, stealing and not stealing, bearing true witness and false witness; it is not a moderate order. The knowledge from which the Ten Commandments came was informed about the sorts of things that people do, but it did not set the standard to accommodate human frailty. It gave weighty laws, laws that conserve the identity of Jews as Jews. The simplest lesson is: consideration for the other person. Upon this, the inhabitants of the earth can agree.

The Ten Commandments want nothing unusual, only respect for the other person, enabling people—as nations, societies, humanity—to live together.

God takes up residence in the consciousness of the individual through the mediation of words and fragments of text, because "you" can be the lonely mortal and it can also be the people who through this law make a covenant with the only and eternal power: so that the people might be long-lived on this earth.

137. Moses helps; he is the interpreter, the one who dares to come closest to the voice speaking from the fire, as it introduces itself: I am that I am. The Almighty Power is who He is, the divine Other, the only "you."

Moses establishes the dialogue, which thereafter manages to continue somehow. He is frail, as are the prophets. The dialogue of frail men with a jealous God, actually a frail God. The dialogue supposes mutual frailty: jealousy supposes love.

Between God and man, between the infinite and the finite, tension is everlasting, alliance is conditional. The validity of the contract is based on the contract's being fulfilled by both parties. Some of the tension is the accusation of God, if brutal events can be interpreted as breach of contract.

Did He go too far? Was He not paying attention? Certain facts leave the perplexed person without a guide. After the twentieth century's bounty of slaughter, in which the killers all conceived of themselves as good patriots, is there still meaning to the words "Do not kill"? Whom do these words bind? God? Man? No one at all?

To see an image of the Almighty in the other person, in our mirror image: it behooves us not to treat that image in a way that we would not like to be treated, because we don't want someone to kill us, to steal from us, to slander us, to seduce our wives, and to envy us perpetually. With its own moral minimalism, this is a possible basis of folk morality. This is the minimum of solidarity necessary for survival. But as we have seen, survival is not completely certain even then.

The Ten Commandments of Moses are the transcultural minimum, the portable moral message you cannot sidestep, the one that pops up under other names, composed differently in every culture. Respect for the other person, yes, this is the essence of the teaching. The rest is just commentary.

1990

Shabbatai Tzvi:
Messiah? Con Man? Artist?

138. There are people who believe that God speaks inside them, that a higher spirit thinks through them. I am not I, I am more than myself. When I open my mouth, celestial authority speaks, please respect and love me. I didn't have an easy childhood, and I am often sad. Sometimes, however, I can be nothing but the sacred lamp itself. This type of reasoning is more frequent among manic-depressive half-wits than in the general population.

There is a citizen of Smyrna, a Mediterranean, a European traveler, knowledgeable enough, a good singer and actor, an improvising surrealist games master who organizes a great wedding, and, weeping with happiness, he dances with his bride—a Torah scroll. He manages to last through two marriages without losing his virginity; he does not touch the good wives delivered to him by the tradition—both marriages end in divorce—and the first woman he embraces is a visionary prostitute, who recognizes at a great distance that he, Shabbatai Tzvi, is the king of the Jews.

Then let us imagine that this unfortunate, psychologically disturbed person, whom Doctor Scholem diagnoses as a sufferer of psychosis or manic-depressive neurosis, turns to an excellent young psychiatrist (an adherent of the Lurian Cabalist school of psychoanalysis), Nathan of Gaza, who bows before him and says: "You are the Messiah."

Is it any wonder that Shabbatai Tzvi believes all the nice things said about him? Others view him as half crazy, at best. He would rather be the Messiah than half crazy.

139. We are all God's children. And who doesn't believe that many are called but few are chosen, and that he, Shabbatai Tzvi in this instance, happens to be one of the few? Reserved Cabalists spoke of certain reclusive messiahs, so reclusive indeed that neither others nor they themselves knew of their identity. God was content to be the only one who knew.

If a person lives in the time of waiting—let's say before 1666, on the threshold of the apocalyptic turn, when everyone waits for something—if, for example, the spirit of the Cabala has touched them, they wait for God to return to his condemned human beings, to the earth from which he withdrew and left open to the conflict between good and evil.

140. A theatrical talent now gets an idea: the reclusive God's message should not only shine in red on the blade of a saber slicing off a neck, not only shine in the triumph or ruin of the gladiators, it should also appear as baroque theater, on decorated galleys, in the framework of holidays and academies. Let the great Messiah show begin!

What can the Messiah do? Speak cleverly? He should leave that to the doctors. Fight? Leave that to the soldiers. He sings psalms. Texts are provided by Nathan, the youthful Cabalist imagemaker; he will be Paul beside Shabbatai. Not afterward, but now. Standing right beside him. Don't talk too much, just sing, I'll do the talking.

141. We might think Nathan was the cold strategist beside the manic-depressive Shabbatai. But we do not think it. If Nathan was cold, why did he believe the sultan would yield when he saw the splendor of Shabbatai, that nice, big, fat man, that red-nosed, sparkling-eyed one, with his carefully trimmed full beard? If Nathan was cold, why did he believe that after the sultan heard the master sing, he would get off his throne and put the King of the House of Israel upon it and say to him, "Please, you sit here, because this place is for you." The young Nathan was too deeply affected by his studies; he thoroughly overvalued the power of the psalms. Serious scholars, people experienced in seafaring, commerce, and finance, authors and publishers—all shared Nathan's illusions. It was a tribute to his talent and that of Shabbatai. They were a good pair, Shabbatai and Nathan, the mystical illusionists. Their performances were successful—proving that their contemporaries needed this spectacle. It was in the air, a feeling that the miracle, the turn, some long-expected unexpectedness was imminent.

142. There was no serious Jewish messianic experiment until Shabbatai Tzvi fever, except once: Bar Kochba, with Rabbi Akiba, the man of the spirit, on his side. This was the armed uprising, the popular revolution against the empire. It did not succeed; they were killed. Akiba asked those who set him on fire to water the flames from time to time, so that his immolation would last longer; he did not want to hurry the last prayer.

The first, successful experiment may also be mentioned, the one by the Essene dissident of Nazareth, an early Tolstoyan. Do not resist evil by force. A condemned Jew stands up for his word by dying on the cross. Jewish intellectuals were crucified by the thousands in those days. Martyrdom as salvation, the rabbi in place of you, once and for all. The sacrifice was transferred to Jesus. Salvation is invisible; it will not be yours in this world, only on the other side.

143. Some Jews were not content with faith in the saving cruci-fixion of another man. They believed in survival, because they knew that that wasn't easy either. Thus their symbol is the patri-arch, the older man with a large family, or perhaps with a kingdom, with the sensuality of the Song of Songs and the relentless clear-sightedness of Ecclesiastes. The experienced man rather than the beginner. In the end, Moses, the lawgiver. The one who wants to elevate the Jews and make them a priestly people by separating the divine from the human, by rejecting every anthropomorphic de-piction of God. For someone with this sensitivity, the deification of a corpse is an unacceptable concession. The schism took place, the two religions were separated, to their mutual misfortune.

144. In what could the Jews trust after they had been expelled from Spain and massacred on Ukrainian and Polish soil? Zion-ism had not yet emerged. The Jews of Jerusalem were poor; they even asked master Shabbatai to go and collect money on their behalf from the rich Jews of Alexandria. Later, the Shab-bataians' undertaking was sponsored by a rich Amsterdam Jew. Alexandria and Amsterdam were rich places; Jerusalem was a poor place.

Trouble, and lots of it, was a permanent condition, as was the need for something to happen. Some kind of nonarmed action. The Jews needed some new "good news": the story of the evan-gel, the crucifixion, the sacrifice was not happy enough.

145. Well then? Let's act as if it were true. Should we believe that a band of hippies will dazzle the Mediterranean region on a motley fleet of boats? Should we believe that the hearts of rulers can be moved by deep sayings, psalms, and celebrations condon-ing even free love? Did they really believe? Did serious people believe? It is a fact that they would have liked very much to be-lieve. The Shabbataian adventure was the great, grotesque delir-ium of the Jews.

146. Come on over here, you celebrity, the sultan says to Shabbatai. The messiah's entourage landed in the hopes that the master would convert the sultan.

"Either put on this turban, or I'll have your head cut off. You decide!" Shabbatai donned the turban and kept it on when he rejoined his faithful, who were waiting at the gate.

They beat him, spit on him, abandoned him—but not all of them. Some interpreted the events as the saint's having to endure the sin of self-denial, the mortal sin, apostasy, in order to preserve the chance of starting anew. The other remaining faithful accepted the notion of a frail messiah. For a while.

147. Tragicomedy in search of an author. Though attracted to Jewish mysticism, Professor Scholem applies the strictness of the scholar or perhaps the rabbinical moralist to this story of great baroque con-artistry and impostors. Its unique beauty was that so many people believed in it.

Most likely there won't be any more Jewish messiahs for a long while. This last experiment also ended in comedy. Would the piece have been better if Shabbatai had had his head cut off?

For Shabbatai, the turban was actually only a costume. He favored strange, varicolored dress; why not wear that of the Muslims—out of kindness, even? But then which headdress isn't a costume? Have you ever seen a noncostume hat?

The others have petty reservations, of course, but they cannot expect the master to imitate Jesus! He sings wearing various hats, when he feels like singing; he still draws an audience, and he stays in one piece.

148. I like this colleague. "Poor friend of mine, why did you have to play messiah?" On second thought, I say, "You did well to play it!" Then, "And you were clever to refuse the alternative of losing your head and thus obtaining a little afterlife for yourself."

Such frailty does not stop us from feeling sympathy. This poor, sick, but certainly talented clown was our last messiah.

149. This was the last religious experiment that was able to bring many in the house of Israel to rapture. Then came the tzaddiks, and Doctor Kafka and his ilk, but these were unique instances of transcendence. The seventeenth century was still an age for mystical sailing, for rapture to spread in a network, for faith in the present as the appointed time, the time of fulfillment, and it was an age for faith in our ability to recognize the Messiah, even to be the ones who single him out, in the form of this large man who behaves strangely. Because the message really is there, in his enigmatic sayings, in the words of his spokesmen, in the singing, dancing sailors. Yes, that *now*, that seduction and being seduced was the great time. The fact is, many believed the Jews had a king who triumphed by singing and not killing.

150. It was such an enjoyable story that it was worth believing for a while. Then, once it became more ambiguous, more complex, realistic Jewish literature might have begun, more or less in Cervantes's time. Like Don Quixote, Shabbatai Tzvi also undertook the impossible. Early absurd heroes.

151. I can imagine Heine would have been interested in the figure of Shabbatai Tzvi. But Jewish authors made real attempts at ironic, worldly metaphysics only in the twentieth century, two to three hundred years later. In their mythology, a special place should be allotted to the frail messiah, the artist-colleague, Shabbatai Tzvi, in whose defense the next International PEN World Congress would surely send a telegram to the sultan. Shabbatai Tzvi would not be censured for converting to the Muslim faith. The sultan was relatively merciful: once Shabbatai put on the turban, he was allowed to live in Istanbul.

Letter to the Former Prisoners of Buchenwald

152. I bow my head in respect simply because you were there. Having been sent there is itself a sign of moral merit. Those imprisoned there were under suspicion of being good, of having done something against tyranny, and of having done it in the name of freedom, even if the word has been interpreted in many different ways.

Brotherhood among people can never be perfect. The brotherhood of victims lined up against the wall is certainly better than that of the firing squad.

That you meet to remember together, in spite of your advanced age, proves the solidarity of former camp dwellers. Your former guards probably do not meet. The captivity you survived through the mercy of fate (also through endurance and cooperation) only proves that you were the ones who adhered to truths that were dangerous then, that you bore the special nature that was condemned to death then.

I respect those condemned to death and those who stayed alive, Jews and Christians, the religious and those without religion, people whom dictatorship put behind barbed wire for their political convictions.

153. The sufferings of the camp dweller are not enough to ensure a straight path to truth. The fact is, no straight path leads to the truth; a labyrinth of mistakes leads there.

Those who were there learned something, but they did not become repositories of truth from that experience alone. They shared in one truth. They looked into the face of fascism. They understood the connection between fascist rhetoric and the machinery of annihilation.

154. The methods used in the mass destruction of innocents are not a question of primary importance. From gas to clubs to starvation, there are many ways to kill, ways that range from frenzied to indifferent.

The fact of primary importance: People can be killed just for being who they are. For being different. For being Jews. For being democrats. For being Communists. For telling a joke. For having given someone refuge. For not having reported someone. For not having been a traitor.

155. I know there were Communists at Buchenwald. I also know they organized and helped one another survive by infiltrating the prisoner hierarchy, most likely at the expense of non-Communist prisoners.

I also know that many former prisoners do not want to acknowledge that there were also concentration camps in the Soviet Union; moreover, that some of those camps, in the name of the struggle against fascism or imperialism, approved or even helped bring about the execution or imprisonment of people—for being democrats, for being Communists in a different way, for telling a joke, for being who they were.

There were those who did not commit such acts, who opposed them instead. But perhaps they approved of aggressive acts against others—not criminals, just members of a community branded an enemy.

156. States declared guilty respectable people who did not hurt others collectively, and states tried to destroy them just because those people belonged to one or another ethnic, religious, societal or political group—this was the great degeneracy of the twentieth century.

This century brought back into fashion the barbarian idea of general guilt, so that people could be hated in an organized fashion just because they belonged here or there, so that on the basis of simple-minded classifications and categorizations a white-gloved hand could send someone to the right or to the left, summarily sentencing an individual to death or temporary survival, and the decision would be not about the person but about a cliché, an abstract conceptual image in the minds of those possessing armed power. That mass graves and crematoriums come from abstractions should prompt all of us to rethink, every year, the events that took place then.

157. Those who send people to concentration camps think up many word pictures for certain groups of their fellow humans, pictures of the members of those groups not as people but as animals and, within the category of animals, as insects or even less.

Nazism was the ideological withdrawal of empathy. You cannot empathize with the prisoner, because he is, strictly speaking, not a person. The official Bolshevik revolutionary was also obligated to deny empathy for prisoners, because the prisoners were not humans but monsters and rotten ones at that. If we think back to these two examples of a reduction that deprives people of human rank in the name of justice for a nation or class, what stands out is the primitiveness of the reasoning—I might say, its stupidity.

We see that it is still possible to hate and destroy in an organized fashion in the name of one nation or another. Those who shoot in the name of their nation today are all convinced of their rightness, and they are very insulted when others find them similar to one another.

158. In the camp prisoner I see the victim treated in a way that should not be allowed. The fascist camps were unique in that they killed children using the methods of mass production. That was not characteristic of the Gulag. The child suffocated by gas is the ultimate victim, and the mass annihilation of Jewish children was the ultimate crime of the century; compared to it, all other organized killing is less.

The other kinds of killing were awful, but this was the most awful. When I see a small child, sometimes that image of death comes to me, with an inner fade to darkness.

159. My respect goes to the prisoner who returned home and did not assist in the imprisonment of others. Because if the passion for justice swings like a pendulum, always punishing newer victims, then revenge bounces here and there like a tennis ball, making frail people prisoner and jailer alternately.

I bow my head before all my fellow humans, because they all have the victim in them. Because no one is without fear of death.

I do not bow my head before the perpetrators, even if they were victims in an earlier part of their lives.

160. Glorying in wrongs suffered is a phenomenon I've viewed with suspicion, as it occurs with every political turn and change of regime.

An atmosphere favorable to the commission of newer crimes, goading actors to self-satisfied imbecility: that is triumphalism. When outrageous deeds take place in our neighborhood, let us look inward in dread. We might have got mixed up in it too, as in an accident on the highway.

161. Those who were there may have come to understand how not to treat their fellow humans. Most former camp dwellers probably wished for a country in which there were no camps, for themselves and for others. Camps being built and people being put in them cannot happen in a democratic Europe. There are places where it is still possible, and there the local leaders have cause to be anxious; infamy may await them.

When the former prisoners celebrate their liberation, they should spare no effort in their study of camp philosophy and camp psychosis.

The reliable country is one in which concentration camps never existed, do not exist now, and are not even possible.

Whether a society has been cured of the disease of enclosing fellow humans into camps can be established only after the passage of time, a long quarantine.

1993

The Permanently Waiting

162. The question: Can Jews stay in Central and Eastern Europe? Between 80,000 and 100,000 Jews live in Hungary, about 20,000 in Romania, thousands in the other countries of the region. The Jews of Central Europe had the opportunity to emigrate in several waves; many did leave, the overwhelming majority in some places. In Hungary, more than half of those who stayed alive emigrated.

Those who stayed made a decision to stay. Perhaps the aged were kept back by fear of being left stranded, but the aged of today were not aged after the war. There is no wave of emigration today either, no aliyah comparable to that of Soviet Jews. Some young scientists and highly qualified professionals undertake work elsewhere, quietly, as if in a temporary sojourn.

The vast majority of Central European Jewry waits. It waits to see what will happen. If there will be constitutional democracy in Central Europe, if the relationship of the state to individuals and minority groups will be liberal, if society tolerates plurality, being

Written answer to a question posed by a Dutch liberal Jewish periodical. I read a part of it at a conference in January 1994.

itself increasingly a coat of many colors, then the Jews will stay. If these things do not come to pass, then the number of Jews will dwindle, or they may even leave in a wave.

True, even if most leave, there will always remain a few, and it will be difficult to reduce those few to none. A few will stay to guard the prayer house, the cemetery, the written memories of Jewish presence in Central and Eastern Europe.

163. The answer to the question depends primarily not on the Jews but on the environment. The Jewish question is not the Jews' question. The Jews are not in question. The question is not whether they want to stay here. Those who wanted to leave were able to leave. Those who stayed wanted to stay. They were kept here not by external force but by inner choice. The question is not what the Jews are like. The question is about the environment, the majority: is it integrative or exclusive?

The question is not whether the Jews find Central and Eastern Europe suitable; it is, rather, whether the region will cast them out again. The question is: Will political anti-Semitism come into fashion again, or will the region accept the Western, democratic community of values?

If it does accept those values, it will not endeavor to construct a historical continuity that glosses over the extermination of the Jews and discusses it as a not really characteristic feature of the pre-1945 regime. The moral laundering of the environment of deportation is unacceptable to the Jews. Is there anyone we can expect to understand and retroactively forgive the partial or complete liquidation of his family? The rehabilitation of the Nazi satellite regimes means the upward valuation of prefascism and its atmosphere, one in which the series of Jewish laws was possible.

The European radical right readily returns to family-ethnic origin, in other words, to the concept of race. Neo-Nazism makes a comeback on the margins, and European anti-Jewishness pairs with the anti-Jewishness of Islamic extremists. If all European nations wish to restore the uninterrupted continuity of their own history, then anti-European nationalism will have to look back approvingly on Hitlerism, since fifty years ago almost all of Europe was under German rule.

164. This society is now learning the possibility of living in more than one way. The dominant tendency is pluralism rather that homogenization. Now comes worry over falling apart, decay, and the charge that the devilish subverter is responsible for the calamity.

Many kinds of ambition and lifestyle have stepped into the market of possibilities in recent years; there have been violent movements upward and downward. Many kinds of political opportunities are available. There are also many opportunities for criminality and downward mobility. The range spanned by the layers of society has become wider than it was before, and the whole of society has moved from the average toward the unusual.

A diversity of self-conscious minorities has appeared. It is natural that one group of leaders represents minorities only temporarily; soon functionaries arrive, identifying the interests of the minority with their own, rendering it more difficult for the minority to exercise plural choice and make initiatives in several different directions. Discord and disparate orientations appear in organizations of nationalities as well, therefore even the extent to which ethnic politicians represent the interests of individuals belonging to the ethnic minority is unclear.

165. In the cultural-economic sphere, organization and union are not obstructed by anything; Jews have no need for any kind of statutory advantage there. Jews want to be normal, and want to see their obligations clearly, so they can be law-abiding citizens.

It is proper for them to be loyal to the country while free in their domestic political orientation, joining and voting as they wish. The fact that they are Jews means no type of obligation or prohibition for them.

If the dominant spirit is that of the law and civil liberty, the small number of Jews, with their own particularity, will be considered valuable to society. In that case, even Jewish immigration to the big cities of Central Europe is conceivable. In that case, it is worthwhile to consider the alternatives in Jewish behavior. If, however, it becomes necessary for Jews to leave, then their range of choices will obviously be restricted.

166. Here is my answer. I expect democracy to become more stable in the Central European region in this decade, and the opposing option—nationalist dictatorship, which promises not much good for the Jews—not to gain much ground. The rhetoric of the radical nationalist right is not effective on the majority of Central Europeans, nor is hostile propaganda about neighboring countries or ethnic groups, and against the personnel of yesterday's Communist regime, and against the imaginary dragon with three heads. One head is America, the second, simplified, is the World Bank, but the third and most dangerous head is international Jewry. I see neither radical impulses nor passionate irrationality; instead I see reluctant, slightly hopeful people who disdain extremes.

167. All tendencies and ideological trends are revived, none can be buried forever, but none achieves permanent dominance, none is able to install an autocracy of its own, because movement and mutability are great.

Taking into account the many orientations of individuals, the great variability of life strategies in our region, the economic transformation, and the faces of our cities, I hold pluralism to be the chief tendency. Embourgeoisement proceeds along lawful and unlawful channels. Professionalization moves forward; a new middle class is in dynamic formation, as is a new elite, one that is naturally both new and old.

The citizens have obtained certain freedoms, and they don't look kindly on someone's wanting to deprive them of one of these freedoms in the name of any idea. Passionate pluralism does not accommodate new collectivist fashions. Individual roads to success are more interesting to young people than wearing some kind of uniform and chanting slogans. The chief trend continues to be embourgeoisement; sympathy flows mostly toward moderate, predictable, and sober leaders.

168. The Jews left the ghetto, and this cannot be undone. To go forth from the closed community of ritual, from the Jewish feudal organization—this was the great adventure! So much so that they removed the sacred and everyday language, the connection between the ritual and the linguistic-religious. Was this great degree of undressing necessary? Was this not the overenthusiasm of neophytes, of those just emerged from the ghetto?

In any case, Jewry was capable of mixing and of forgetting itself. But when it forgot itself and gave no sign that it was different, it still seemed different. Only Jewry thought it was not different; its environment didn't believe it.

169. Jews too might retain a sense of shame, inasmuch as they followed fashion by participating in the nationalist and Communist experiments in dissolving. They wanted to get rid of their Jewish nature in these movements. Anti-Semitic Jews are as dangerous as can be; restless, they cannot be placed anywhere. On the other hand, many Jews perceive any specific statement about Jews as anti-Semitism.

170. As emancipated Jewry stepped into the Enlightenment and into the modern era, it had no easy task in identifying with

the outstanding qualities of the people in whose environment they lived but not identifying with their prejudices. Thorough reasoning is required to see the diversity of the world and the great relativities of world culture, and at the same time to see that there are fundamental, common moral laws.

Those laws have (among others) Jewish interpretations that have proven durable, but worldly Jewry of today does not exclude other interpretations on its intellectual horizon. The strategy of understanding can advance world integration, since it perceives the beauty of various paths.

171. The western band of yesterday's Eastern Europe impatiently urges integration with Western Europe on all planes, including the military, but it will learn that being dependable entails fulfilling some stiff conditions. Patience and self-restraint, among others. If it will be capable of these as well, then societal consciousness will gradually form an organic connection to the Western community of values. In other words, if Warsaw, Cracow, Prague, Brno, Bratislava, Ljubljana, and Budapest will be open and sparkling big cities, as they are already becoming, then natural traffic (almost independently of the degree of institutional integration) will shape common European norms, and in such an atmosphere Jews too will find their place.

172. The preceding optimistic prognosis applies emphatically to the metropolitan areas mentioned above but with more caution, more anxiousness, and a somewhat later schedule to the region that includes the former Soviet Republics, Romania, and the Balkans.

According to my prognosis, the whirlpool that has come about in former Yugoslavia—we might call it the Bosnia Syndrome—alarms rather than tempts the entire region.

Ethnic civil war needs a mixed ethnic composition between

the mountains and the old guerrilla tradition with its cult of armed men. It does not occur elsewhere or in other ways. If there's something Central European citizens don't want in their neighborhood, its just the sort of thing they've been seeing on the news each night.

The Bosnia Syndrome is not contagious. The Caucasus doesn't take its cues from the Balkans; it started shooting earlier. There are many active movements in the Central European region, but the crazy are in the minority, and the center squeezes the irresponsible out to the margins.

173. Naturally there is and will be a radical right in Central and Eastern Europe. Whether or not it promotes anti-Semitic programs, the logic of its mentality takes it near the sporadically emerging thesis of neofascism. Those drawn to it, those agreeing with it constitute 10 percent of the population at most, but more likely less. In other words, about the same percentage as in larger Western European countries.

In the ex-Soviet countries and in southeastern Europe, political articulation is even less developed than in Central Europe, and here the group receptive to neofascist phraseology fluctuates between one-fifth and one-fourth. It is possible, however, that this shifting mass that searches for its place will slip out from under a modern fascist movement. They are occasional, protesting voters, whose sympathy roves over the political palette.

174. The serious answer to extremism is building up solid, constitutional, parliamentary democracy, and a certain consensus among conservatives, liberals, and socialists on what they will tolerate and what they will not.

Though there is skepticism and disappointed grimacing toward the West, neither the radical right nor the old-new Communists of today can offer anything better than multiparty constitutional democracy and a market economy. Both of the former would like to get a place in Parliament, but to do so they must submit to parliamentary logic and customs.

I don't hold the analogy to Weimar democracy to be realistic: the great landslide to the far right is just phantasmagoria. The story of Nazism alarms the majority just as much as Bosnia does. The major players have learned and are careful; radical-populist enthusiasm is not typical of them; they abstain from supporting neofascist adventures.

175. I am able to appraise the risk of this optimistic prognosis, and the sinister scripts are not unfamiliar to me. I also consider the possibility that the Central Europeans' desire to join will not be accepted by Western Europe within a foreseeable period of time, something that could be grounds for anti-Western resentment, while it also causes confusion of identity: where is it we belong? This refusal could favor a Central European emancipation process, or the reinstatement of authoritarian-etatist structures, with nationalist rather than socialist phraseology this time.

Nationalist phraseology inevitably finds itself confronting the dilemma between regional-political and ethnic-religious national definitions. For Jews, it is clear that the first is not discriminatory while the second becomes so.

For example, if living in Hungary, being a Hungarian citizen, and speaking Hungarian are not enough to make one Hungarian, if there are two other criteria as well—to be Christian and the descendant of an old Hungarian family—and if the definition of Hungarian is lost in the fog of ethnic origin, and if the ethnic (before long: racial) concept of nation achieves a lasting victory over the political concept, sharpening the conflict between majority and minority and producing a religious and suspicious version of nationalism, then Jews will be forced to emigrate from this country. The designation *Hungarian* can of course be replaced by any national adjective in the Central and Eastern European region.

176. The key theme in the collapse of former Yugoslavia, I believe, is that vocal minorities of the national intellectual bureaucracies exchanged the federative, political concept of the Yugoslav nation for their own ethnic-religious, not even cultural-linguistic, concept of nation. The substitution took place in the public media and in the political negotiations, while the West irresponsibly accepted this reversal of priorities, accepted that politicians operating with ethnic-religious legitimization should be able to make nation-states without the contractual agreement of all interested parties.

Everything that has happened in this unfortunate country, all the killing and suffering, I regard as connected to the Yugoslav political classes' view of their collective selves and their nation, and to the ambition that the state should be uniform and homogeneous—with regard to ethnicity, religion, and language—because it's nicer that way. Better than being bigger and many colored is staying small but at least monochromatic.

I could say that there's a tendency in Eastern Europe to get stuck on the ethnic-religious self. But if I think of Northern Ireland, the elections in Antwerp, Italian separatism and neofascism, or if I consider that neo-Nazi-type violent acts and views are no more rare in the western part of Germany than in the eastern part, then we can say that the regions of Europe, to varying degrees but in general, are uncertain of how to interpret their own concepts of nation, the basis for deciding who they consider one of them and who they consider strangers.

177. One of the advantages of European integration is that these dilemmas lose much of their dramatic force, rendering impossible the typical case in former Yugoslavia: if a child is born of

a mixed marriage, he or she has to decide between mother and father, because the issue of ethnic identity has become the primary one, an eventuality that the carefree young couple didn't imagine, even in their worst dreams, at the time of their nuptials.

The other advantage of European integration is that the various collectives are compelled just by etiquette to see themselves in a wider frame and to limit their narcissism. This behavior inevitably accompanies the acceptance of multicultural society and the aesthetic of the plural personality. The logic of European integration favors the political-territorial concept of nation, which can be in concord with linguistic-cultural and ethnic-religious communities' being considered special and valuable flowers of the European Community, even if they do not have an independent army.

If European integration somehow works despite its inherent difficulties, then Jews are normal anywhere within an integrated Europe. If there was a European citizenry-bourgeoisie that dreamed of such a Europe at the turn of the century and between the two wars, it was the Jews, until the arrival of Hitler's new Europe, in which the Jews no longer had a place.

178. The political state, constitutional patriotism, and civic consciousness based on the European or, as it were, Atlantic community of values are unquestionably modern and rational creations. They do not grow like weeds from the soil of the historical past. Out of the soil of the past, however, does grow the coexistence of national communities and their engaging in the most diverse neighbor-family symbioses, if the directors of public opinion do not incite them against each other. But the directors do incite them, planting the anxieties "we've been left to ourselves" and "we're abandoned," especially if the developments in international relations strengthen this impression.

179. The Central European elites must also consider the prospect that full membership in the European Community will

be postponed for an unforeseeable amount of time. In that case, establishing institutional forms of Central European cooperation is a meaningful measure that may be of much use later.

Central European cooperative organization of this sort could establish partner relationships with other regional associations in the world. Among the smaller nations and peoples between the two great nations, the German and the Russian, institutional co-operation could create the kind of emotional familiarity that can be sensed in the northwestern European democracies, where the spirit of autonomy has combined with the practice of rational contracting.

180. European integration in the not too distant future would be best. Separate Central European integration is less desirable. Least desirable is the psychological condition of being left alone as a nation, surrounded by an environment believed unfriendly, hostile, or even menacing.

This prospect must also be taken into account, and is unpleasant for Jews, because for the majority it encourages national definition along ethnic-religious lines and the warlike worldview that regards another ethnic-religious group as an a priori fifth column.

The name of the minority is practically a matter of indifference: it can be Jewish, Hungarian, Serbian, Croatian, Muslim, or Christian. The common essence is geopolitical neurosis. Remaining alone would be a great trial for a community and might result in the emigration of its remaining Jews in great numbers.

Without lies and slaughter it was not possible to eradicate the Jew from Central Europe. It was not possible to eradicate the memory of former owners and occupants of ethnically cleansed houses. Violent operations using military-governmental instruments (fired up by exclusive nationalist puppets) to obstruct the coexistence of different peoples are not enough to eradicate the memories of those who once lived there. Uneasy consciences remain. Guilt that cannot be processed.

181. There is a chance that both European and Central European integration will be adopted as a goal by the inhabitants of the region, and in this hopeful atmosphere, in this large-scale European project, the Christian environment can consider Jews competent and dependable partners. This idea has not yet been taken off the agenda.

I consider the optimistic scenario more probable than the defeatist one. Partly out of habit—I regarded the bloc system named Yalta as a passing phantom when it did not seem to be such in the eyes of the majority. And partly because I think societal-cultural processes, in this case embourgeoisement and cultural pluralization, are wider and more influential than the interests of a particular ideological wing of a national bureaucracy.

182. The extreme right wing nurtures itself on national loneliness and the hysteria that comes from being fenced in. As I have stated, the majority has no need for this. But learning democracy takes time. Central Europeans have won much and lost much; they have gone through significant societal transformation without violence. Peace three kilometers from the Yugoslav border, and the people there not angry with one another, is at least as big an achievement as peace in the Netherlands, where the people are not angry with one another.

Discounting what must be discounted—Bosnia and the Caucasus, places of great mixings and the establishment of new nations, where the need of ethnic-religious communities for political self-determination has led almost inevitably to bloody conflicts—Central Europe is basically a peaceful part of the continent, though it suffers from the crisis of system transition.

183. All of the anxieties the Western subconscious likes to transfer to the half-barbarian neighbors outside the city walls—mass migration, organized crime, the horrific images of wild extremism run rampant—they either never happened or happened in less

than dramatic proportions. Czechoslovakia split in two peacefully, and the other nations can be called more or less stable, established, working well or not so well. All parties concerned consider their borders a given and do not dispute them. Providing appropriate rights to ethnic-cultural-religious-linguistic minorities will be a long project; however, it must be carried out in such a way that the majority is not driven wild by nightmare images of secession and civil war.

184. There are neofascists, but they can be combated, and their bulletins are not sold in great numbers. Fascist newspapers may be produced legally in the United States too, but as their audience is small, most consider them a virus that may be allowed to exist because the immune system of the organism can handle it.

As neofascism already appears in almost every European country, there is foundation for speaking of an international fascist network. Similar people are glad of each other's company, and though they rail against each other too, they have a common ground and a common interest.

Inasmuch as international fascism attempts to replace democratic institutions with dictatorship, inasmuch as it creates paramilitary organizations, inasmuch as it commits arson and violent crimes, inasmuch as it stockpiles arms, and inasmuch as it sounds slogans and distributes texts that incite people to violence, it must be the object of police action, just like left-wing terrorism, just like any kind of destabilizing international terrorism.

185. Promoting democratic development in the region east of the former Iron Curtain is in the interest of the West. If the region's "Westerners" suffer cultural-economic and political defeat once again, if democracy brings only misery for the majority, if the West allows or encourages the creation of third-world conditions in Eastern Europe, then half-crazy charlatans will emerge with fascist rhetoric and unpredictable control of the nuclear arsenal.

If there is no democratic global strategy, the world will be a risky place, and the mistake will be paid for later. Wherever fascism is in the offing, anti-Semitic rhetoric becomes more forceful and is always accompanied by anti-Western irrationality. An increase in anti-Jewish references and allusions therefore can almost be regarded as a thermometer reading.

186. Anti-Semitic neofascist rhetoric must be taken seriously as a societal illness, because it can cause great and violent problems. The mass murder of World War II was preceded by the kneading of anti-Semitic rhetoric. The rhetoric prepared the environment to approve extermination of the Jews as parasites. Violent speech is usually followed by violent actions.

It sometimes seems comical to marshal constitutional arguments against the vulgar curses in anonymous letters, with their demand that the addressee get lost if he knows what's good for him, to Israel or wherever, it doesn't matter, just away from here, because his presence here is unbearable.

187. Anti-Semites imagine some kind of secret information network connects Jews and that Jews concert their actions through it. There is an easily offended niche, not very large but not inconsequential, that would like to "rise up" against the Jews. They cannot be convinced, won over, or brought into reasonable dialogue, because their passions come before their judgments of reason, because empathy and hatred do not face each other in their souls. If we want to stay here, our task is to win agreement on fair and decent coexistence not from them but from the majority that designates these extremists' place in the game.

188. As long as the trend is westward, the Jews will not be bothered. If they are really equal, they can stay here. Central European neobourgeois societies probably will place legality ahead of ideologies; they will want to conform to European discipline; and

they will attach decreasing importance to one of the fundamental issues of the folk/urban, populist/Western, nationalist/democratic antinomies: in this region, in this homeland, can there be, should there be Jews too?

189. Should we leave a place where we are called undesirable by some and sometimes by many? Or should we found a school there? I have decided to be a Jew in my own way in this place that has been both given and, in the course of life, chosen. I write this by candlelight. The electricity of the village has gone out in the snowstorm. I will stay where I was born and raised, where my family has worked respectably for centuries. I hold waves of violence to be transitory.

190. It might be said that survival is at stake in the match between the Jews and those who hate them. One must be constantly alert; the one who makes a mistake loses. Whether they want it or not, Jews are in a societal contest, not just as citizens or according to their professions but also on the basis of their religion and family origin.

In most nation-states there is or can emerge a discriminatory mood that rejects a particular racial-religious-cultural minority. This rejection becomes the means of livelihood for a radical group, which develops it into an ideology of racial-ethnic-national-religious purity, the ideal of homogeneity. Those who have chosen this path most likely will arrive at anti-Semitism, and will develop that into a passion. Yes, Jew baiting can become a habit, anti-Semitism can grow into an addiction. It becomes a disease of obsession when the patient's brain must always wind up back there, when every subject brings to mind those devilish Jews.

191. If the Jews born here wish to live here, not deformed by anxiety, if they want their country of birth to be their homeland as well, a reliable country, with a future to which their own

hopes are also connected, a country without intent to humiliate them—then the logical goal of Jews with roles in the public sphere will be for the majority and the government to stay within the framework of constitutional democracy. The public good is served in the process, because if the opposite happens, hatred comes to afflict societies, and in the end people hate not just their neighbors but themselves as well.

192. In Central and Eastern Europe, the situation of the Jews is made more difficult by many of their number having taken part in the illegitimate Communist seizure of power. Many Jews participated in the construction of the Party dictatorship. They played active and combatant roles. Their stated reason was the Communist Party's diametrical opposition to Nazism. In 1945, many believed that the Soviet peoples defeated the Germans, in the name of the socialist world ideal, in the name of proletarian internationalism. So that Jews will have no more trouble over their nationality, let internationalism come, let us be proletarians, thought many.

This rhetoric favored poor Jews, little Jews, assistants to shop-keepers, and craftsmen; now suddenly they could lift themselves above their bosses, be promoted to heads of departments at ministries, become directors of large corporations, and from inside their cars they could wave at their nationalized former boss, who now struggled to make a living as a shopkeeper's assistant.

A greater portion of Jews, however, could not take this path, or simply chose not to take it. The greater portion became little people in this system, or stayed little people. There were those who waited for better times, in prison or driven from their homes.

193. And many emigrated from Hungary, the greatest mass in the wave of 1956, but they left before and after 1956 too, continuously if not at a constant rate. Almost all the Jews in Bulgaria left.

In Romania, there were 400,000 after the war; now there are 20,000. Many have left Yugoslavia recently. Most of the few remaining Jews in Poland were compelled to leave in 1969–70.

194. Jews easily fell into the classifications of bourgeois or petit bourgeois. There were Eastern European Communist countries where anti-Semitism grew and started filtering into official policies. The folk anti-Semitism of the cadres broke loose as the nationalist rhetoric of the dictatorship strengthened. In the final decades of Communism, the bureaucracy of the nation-state gradually switched from the phraseology of class struggle to the phraseology of national unity. Official anti-Semitism made its appearance as anti-Zionism. Jews recognized that Brezhnevian Communism was not their affair, and that it was a mistake to have put so much work into Communism. The little Jews who had been elevated looked unambiguously westward, or their children did, who regarded their parents' Marxist clichés as folkloric artifacts.

195. We stand here at a point of intersection. Islam is rising through the Balkans and in Central Asia. The other presence is the large Russian Slavic region penetrating into Siberia. We are justified in feeling that Asia and Europe belong together.

Various dreams are raging here now. One dream is the coincidence of ethnicity and state authority. It would not be fair to say that we do not understand such dreams, since the Western European nations actually became what they are now in the same way; they became largely ethnically homogeneous because of policies directed toward that goal.

The formation of nations has been an unbroken process over the last two centuries, and we have no cause to suspect that it has reached an end. In the talk of new nations, the demand for national unity around one leader and his team is sounded, and those not a part of that unity are in all certainty against it; in other words, they are enemies. The convulsions in this process are generally unfavorable for minorities and thus for Jews.

196. Jews are diverse. There are many kinds of Jewish behavior; each individual isolates, legitimizes, explains a particular life strategy. Jewish behavior is so variable that every general statement regarding Jews is either trivial or ideological in a way that may be friendly or unfriendly. We find examples of everything, and the opposite of everything.

I don't know anyone who has led his life the way I have. And I could go into detail on the particularity of each of my Jewish friends, and my Christian friends, equally. But defining what the minority is like is not even the question; one can't say anything valid about that, just as one can't say anything valid about the majority.

The question is how the majority treats the minority. How does the majority react to this part of the nation that becomes organic, assimilates, but nevertheless remains undissolved? The question is, how problematic is the particularity of Jews for the majority, and how problematic is the majority's inability to place them easily?

197. When anger flares up, every achievement of Jews is only oil on the flames. Let us suppose that the Jews become outstanding in the very thing most valued by the majority people: from the Jew hater's standpoint, they are that much more unsympathetic. They're here, they're there, they advance even when squeezed out; if they are pushed out here, they pop up there. The Jew steps from one language into another, associates with other peoples but does not disappear without a trace inside those nations. Any chameleon-like endeavor at assimilation by the Jew will be rejected sooner or later by some power.

The Jews: a continuous question mark, because they were the ones who did not desire to and could not assimilate completely, because something special remained in them. The assimilation of Slavs and Germans is somewhat easier. Those who assimilate unconditionally are usually those for whom melting into the environment is—elevation. Those who do not feel that their own background holds less value than that of the environment do assimilate, but only partially. Is there a core in Jews that is not dissolvable? Why do they insist on distinguishing themselves from others? And isn't this consciousness of being chosen a provocation that is punished incessantly?

198. Perhaps it is vexing that there is a spiritual-intellectual tradition behind them, an emotional community that spreads over the globe. All nations like to daydream of some kind of national religion, which they try to find in their own philosophical ideas and literature. They want their existence to be doubled in its essence. In the modern age, this type of conjunction doesn't usually work anymore, the artificial unification of the national and the religious, or the dissolving of the religious into the national. There is no tradition behind it, the effort is too obvious; and because it resembles a fashion, it does not last. In contrast, the ambivalence of a tradition of several thousand years—interpretable in many ways—the inseparability of body and spirit can even be thought of as a natural given, which has its reward and its punishment.

199. For the majority, Jews' not being Christians causes tension from the outset. If Christianity is the ruling idea, obviously it is the best one. But then why does this minority stick to some dark secret? Truly, why aren't Jews Christian, why are Jews Jews? Because while mixed marriage and sexual mixing occur, Jewish consciousness returns, even in those of mixed origin. The Jewish

part ferments in the non-Jew; it is an active part of self-consciousness. What is it the Jew insists upon? Why doesn't he melt in entirely?

Those who think that Jews' being "overrepresented" in one or another group is not in order, an anomaly that must be stopped, those who think that the proportion of Jews here or there is a political rather than a cognitive question... are anti-Semites. Those who promote quotas want the *numerus clausus*.

Anti-Semitism serves many ends. Jewry may be used as an explanation for one's failure in life. There is the fear of being left behind. Before, Marxism was predisposed in favor of Jews; from now on, it will be capital. A feeling as ancient as anti-Semitism does not go away.

The anti-Semites say to Jews: Either assimilate or regard yourselves as a national minority whose home is Israel, to where you may as well return. From this point of view, the succession of anti-Semitic anonymous letters is rational: go back to Israel. Normal chauvinism. To make the Jew understandable, categorizable. "Go across the Danube," they say to Hungarians in Slovakia, though only a few say it, and only the more crazy Slovaks; a Hungarian from Transylvania or Novi Sad can get the same treatment. In the case of both Jew and Hungarian, "Go away" is said to people whose ancestors have lived there for centuries. Frequently, those who urge assimilation or uncover false assimilants struggle with the same problem themselves.

200. Central Europe too is a vision of integration, if it exists at all. Within it, every minority is a treasure, and the Vend, the Armenian, and the Jew are at home; in a word, every person is at home there, just for existing, regardless of what is written on his birth certificate, regardless of the circumstances of his birth, for which circumstances he deserves neither credit nor blame.

Even if the fluff of Central European rhetoric is blown away, the actual relationships will remain, the flea markets, the traffic among intelligentsias that has no need of ideology; the collectors will stay, quietly coming, going, and striking up friendships as they need. This is the work that makes latent cultural confederation real, and any other type of political consolidation will be only a derivative of it.

201. There are many metaphors regarding the majority and minority. The "masters," say those on the right, of the majority, because the opposite of the master is the servant or serf. Hosts, or integrating people, say those in the middle. Truly, national liberalism and the liberalism of the nobility emancipated the Jews, and in the second half of the previous century a kind of propriety dictated that politics remain the prerogative of the class historically there first.

This went well enough, until that same class led the country into world war on two occasions. In the first war, Jewish-Hungarian soldiers collected their share of medals for bravery as did Christian-Hungarian soldiers, and sacrificed their young lives on the altar of great European stupidity, a considerable portion of which was built, of human bones, by our homeland, the Imperial and Royal Monarchy. In the second war, Jews and their families received a death sentence from their homeland—from their own state, to which they were loyal. A portion of the young men deported for forced labor had a chance of escaping the sentence; their children and elderly parents did not.

It should be mentioned that a radical minority of young Jews tried to seize political power by revolutionary means, after the historical-traditional elite led the country to catastrophe on two occasions and handed over domestic Jewry to be killed on the second.

Those who have had their families exterminated can believe that they are not safe unless they hold power. Former forced laborers who became state security officers did go wild and behave pathologically, but I do not know of their systematically killing children and the elderly. And in those Eastern European communist regimes with hardly any Jews on their staffs, the level of violence was not lower.

Nevertheless it was a great mistake for young Jews to have taken part in both the 1919 and the post-1945 Bolshevik-type adventures. These decisions were irrational and morally objectionable. After the two wars, young radical Jews were novices as politicians; it would have been better for them not to experiment with something they didn't understand. It was a mistake to undertake the leadership of the nation, the responsibility for the shaping of the lives of millions.

202. What should be the conduct of the Jew of Budapest, Prague, Warsaw, Bucharest, Belgrade, Zagreb, Sofia, Sarajevo? He should do everything possible for the peace of his homeland and environment. He should help to achieve sensible compromises; he should eschew belligerence and not help give simmering tempers form or slogans; he should not stand in the political avant-garde. Even if he is hotheaded, he should train himself to behave more coolly, with more reserve. He should choose understanding and investigation over position taking, decision and the quietly durable over the shrill fly-by-night.

The majority of Central European Jews do not desire the status of national minority, because they have no need for it. They do not wish to isolate, segregate, ghettoize themselves. They do not ask for autonomy—beyond the freedom of association due to all citizens and beyond the rights due to churches. Over and above the requirement that they receive democratic rights, Jewry cannot be considered a single political interest group. It is normal for there to be conservative, liberal, and socialist Jews. There are also extremists, a few. Jews can be and should be diverse. Once the basic freedoms are secured in a country, everyone should follow his own personal road.

203. These days, when it is so natural for children to attend religion classes, an increasing proportion of Jews living outside organized denominations, universalists, Jews without religion, find their way back to a personal brand of Judaism. But why should they preserve a religion that is tied to origin and is genealogically calculated, one maintained as a closed community? A portion of the Jewish intelligentsia has joined in the universal conversation, the conversation that lifts knowledge to the transnational level, where borders are like objects viewed from above, perceived without being restrictive. But doesn't this floating above reality cause uncertainty regarding location?

Each person finds a personal method and the extent to which he will observe the religious rituals. Jews do not want to constitute a political bloc, they vote all over the spectrum, and they are pluralists in the various organizations to which they belong. They cannot stop being the embodiment of "the Jew" to those around them; they cannot stop their behavior from being the basis of positive or negative impressions of Jews in general.

Within the national languages, it would be difficult to determine a succinct stylistic distinction in the speech or literature of Jews. Jews are perhaps unified in their rejection of anti-Semitism. But perhaps not even in this, for there are anti-Semitic half Jews, and three-quarters Jews who try to expurgate the Jewish part of themselves by hating other Jews and inciting people against them.

But someone classified as a Jew according to the Nazi laws cannot forget that classification. It is branded into his mind that he is a Jew, anywhere in the world, in any dress, with any habits, even if he does not solve the mystery of the world with the hypothesis of God and even if he does not acknowledge the limits of his coexistence with others.

204. I stand in a synagogue and leaf through the prayer book on the eve of the Day of Atonement. I'm bored by all this flattery and reverence for the Lord. From the humble point of view, the Lord is a volatile, tyrannical patriarch. Providence either blesses or strikes: it is fatherly. The Jews did not want to put the only son next to the father, because they were all sons who would be fathers one day, according to the nature of things.

What I am doing just now is my practice of religion. They told me as a child that I was an apostate, but I have prayed my whole life long. One might say I am a Jew who believes in God but is without religion.

I do not wish to decide the question of whether I am a Jewish Hungarian or a Hungarian Jew. I can view myself as both, or as neither. When a person sits down to the table, the uniform, costume, identity, and definition should all stay in the foyer on the peg, if possible.

205. If the environment casts a disapproving eye on the Jews, the more cowardly of them to try to disappear into the crowd. To free oneself from the yellow star by submerging into the crowd. And then comes European good taste: don't look to stand out, don't parade your Jewishness, wear it discreetly, like membership in an exclusive club. Sounding off about it makes it less appealing. The person who advertises his trade makes us lose our enthusiasm for the occupation he advertises.

The same goes for religions. Proselytizing cannot be separated from advertising. Jews understand advertising, but they are not proselytizers. Every religion is perfect according to its own inner construction. Religions cannot be broken down and blended together. The citizen establishes his own relation with them, if given the choice, if not forced by great moral and neighborly pressure to choose one or another.

The postmodern point of view particularly favors the renaissance of orthodoxies, and combines anthropological relativism with fashion. In any case, those who choose orthodoxy choose a way of dress. With that freedom of the Western citizen comes the ability to choose. In order to obtain it, bourgeois democracy had to be created, and freedom of religion was a part of it. Feudal organization, military and papal rule, and the closedness of the orthodox community all had to be rejected in the process.

206. If Israel becomes stable, if it becomes an integrating factor in the Near East because the peace process weaves it together with the Arab world, Israel will become increasingly involved in the Near East. But it is also possible that Israel will turn toward Central and Eastern Europe. Some Hungarian Jews living in Israel go back to Hungary, and it is not uncommon now for Hungarian Christians to go to Israel. Hungary has expanding contacts with Israel, and I presume that they will expand more, if only because there are many Hungarians in Israel and many Jews in Hungary.

One can also become habituated to the idea of the Jews as the people of historical Diaspora, in some respects the predecessor of Hungarian destiny, since the Hungarian diaspora is also relatively wide.

207. If the Jews stay here in Central and Eastern Europe, they cannot hide in a hollow; hiding is not the appropriate behavior. The Jews as individuals and as a community must form a repurified and redefined concept of themselves, on the basis of a new honesty.

The duty of the Jew is to formulate his own duty, which should not be in contradiction to the Ten Commandments. He accepts judgment as he is. A person should accept being what he is, and existing as he does. The Lord says, I am that I am. Every Jew who follows the Lord should say the same.

208. The time for religious dialogue between Jews and Christians has come. They have been engaged in dialogue for the longest time, but the religious sphere has been touched on rarely, perhaps because there wasn't lively interest in it until recent times. In order to be able to regard Judaism or Christianity as our own, we must think of them as unfinished, as being shaped by us. We do not identify either religion entirely with the speech of its priests. Everyone who calls himself a Jew or a Christian is entitled to reformulate the meaning of these two words. The free citizen is accountable to God for his religion. We must visit each other's churches and houses. Being frail is allowed. Only the master is not ashamed of being as curious as a child.

1993

Neither Forbidden
nor Prescribed

209. Our human dignity cannot exist without spiritual-intellectual freedom: to believe or not believe in God, according to our own perception.

The inalterable prerequisite for freedom of conscience is that no man, regardless of rank, title, or office, should be able to prescribe what I am allowed to think about the human and the superhuman, about our sphere of vision and that which is beyond it.

Neither government nor religious authority may exercise compulsion or inflict punishment on our consciences. One purpose of democracy is to prevent the state from taking advantage of its extraordinary power: the monopoly over lawful instruments of compulsion. Democratic constitutions declare that the state is not authoritative in questions of religious truth, faith, and conviction.

The modern person removed his body and thinking from the allied authority of church and state. To prevent people from being tortured as heretics, the civil emancipation expressed in constitutions (the spirit of the laws) separated spiritual and physical power.

Certainly, priestly and military authority were connected for millennia. Their separation is a modern phenomenon, accepted in Western civilization only since the era of the Enlightenment. By now the separation of power is almost axiomatic, a fundamental principle no longer really debated.

Does the state have any business or authority over the feelings, beliefs, or thoughts of its citizens? According to Western mentality, it does not; according to Eastern mentality, it does. If the head of state automatically becomes head of the church, or if the head of the church automatically becomes the head of state, if the party leader is considered the wisest of the wise, or if the head of the ideological, indoctrinating party is the sole possessor of government power, then a person can get into trouble for believing and thinking differently.

210. Domains of spiritual liberty cannot be separated from one another; if you injure them here, they will wilt there too; every restriction accepted sets a precedent that can justify the introduction of further restrictions.

Not just the intelligentsia but every thinking citizen has a basic interest in accepting the principle that beliefs and disbeliefs, suspicions and doubts, mystical experiences and scientific convictions should, like poetry, not be subject to supervision by the community-state.

This thesis is conventional in Western-type democracies; in authoritarian regimes, it is not. For theocratic leaders it is not absurd to sentence the novelist to death for a few paragraphs—using violation of religious statutes as legal justification. In the eyes of democrats, such a sentence is idiotic.

211. The possessors of physical power understandably wish to legitimize their rule with religious authority—let's say it, with God. The possessors of spiritual power are understandably willing to endorse the legitimacy of the government, if in exchange the government grants them a monopoly over souls. The alliance

is advantageous to both parties. They reinforce each other's positions.

Rulers need religious legitimization if democratic-constitutional legitimization falters. Tyranny must invoke either God or historical necessity if it wants to stand on its feet, if it wants to silence those who would judge it, those who would raise the issue of the sovereignty of citizens.

The alliance of church and state exempts both parties from the efforts of competition, or at least it secures a better competitive position for them. Because if God doesn't openly favor one politician over the others, then nothing remains but free choice, in which one can win or lose. Similarly, if there is no state religion, churches too must compete for the hearts of the faithful.

212. Modern societies flood their members with choices, inundating them with spiritual advice, forms of thought and feeling, to such an extent that only about a sixth or a seventh of the population attends church, and the competition is basically for this minority.

The majority of people believe in God in their own way, or perhaps don't even believe; at any rate, they do not require the mediation of priest and ritual community between themselves and the truth. It is not surprising, therefore, that the various priestly communities and churches would like to spread their influence to those who believe in their own way, to believers in other religions, and to nonbelievers, but only a fraction of the people in these three categories are potential converts, so it is in the vital interest of churches to hang on to the members they already have.

213. The state built upon religious ideas as its justifying principle is a destructive menace to free education. The same can be said of the state built upon ideological principles, the modern,

worldly variant of the religious state, with recent appearances in the form of radical nationalism (i.e., fascism) and radical social- ism (i.e., communism). An institution integral to the creation of religious and ideological states is censorship (hard or soft), along with inquisition. The ritual of book burning is another attribute of states built upon ideology.

The state of law has no basis other than the free contracts of in- dependent citizens who have formed associations and parties. Idea or contract? That is the question here, the question of freedom.

Naturally, limiters of freedom will all stress the preeminent universality of the ideas in their possession, as opposed to the particular and therefore subordinate interests of the competing- negotiating-contracting parties. Naturally, they will find adver- tising experts among "men of the spirit." The road to slavery is paved with appeals to the soul.

The previous regime in Hungary, the era of state socialism, was the era not only of belligerent atheism but also of secular- ization, if only because the compulsory dissemination of the official worldview engendered spontaneous resistance, which sometimes took the form of a bourgeois aspiration for the beliefs of individuals to be their private affair, free of interference from others.

214. There is no convincing reason for minors not to be en- titled to freedom of thought. Since the interests of children are represented by parents until the children reach maturity, since legal representation for minors does not yet exist, parents have the final say about the sort of education minors receive.

Who is the primary authority with regard to a child's image of the world, the parent or someone else—the pedagogue or the priest, for example? The question is especially interesting if one considers that church attendance is not mandatory but school attendance is. If the school is denominational, and the teaching of every subject is under the direction of the church, then parents compel their child to learn a religious worldview when they register the child voluntarily. If, however, there is no possibility of choice, if parents are under pressure to register children at a religious school beyond any need they might feel for their child to receive religious instruction, then the child is compelled to adopt a religious worldview, under the duress not of parents but of grades.

I regard a child's freedom of choice as a primary value. A child must know that the world may be viewed in more than one way, and that becoming an adult entails preparation to make rational choices. The parent and the professional educator should cooperate in this preparation, so that by the time the child reaches maturity, the talent for freedom emerges, the sovereign person.

215. There is nothing more sobering for a writer than recognizing the right of readers to read his book or not to read it, and if they have read it, either to put it among the readings judged lasting or to put it among those deemed forgettable, and one may view the relationship between chaplains and the faithful the same way.

I have never made a secret of my opinion that the texts spoken of as sacred are literature and that their writers are human-sized colleagues, sometimes geniuses and sometimes not. The protagonists, carriers of sacred truth, I regard to be figures in novels.

I've found that priests of various religions are like my high school teachers, whom I esteemed greatly. I honored my teachers by acknowledging their authority, to the extent of the wisdom I found manifested in them. Even today I do not rebel against what I accepted and learned from them.

I hold the words of priests regarding the divine to be no more and no less valid than the words of literature teachers on literature. Both are intellectuals with diplomas, which isn't everything, though it's better than nothing. But, then, I'm in the same category myself. The story of a person's religious sensibility coincides with his biography; it is an open thing, in progress until his death.

If I accept competition as a writer, I see no reason why teachers, priests, or politicians should exempt themselves from it. I know of churches that are always full because outstanding priests give services there.

216. I've chosen the physical and spiritual-intellectual integrity and inviolability of the human individual as my foremost value. I could have chosen the good of one or another state, of a religious, political, or cultural community, as represented by those who depict it within an institutional context. The representatives of collective good are wont to derive their authority and power from a higher value, one beyond the human, the individual, and the personal. I could have chosen one of these, but I did not. I cannot choose more than one primary value, lest I choose confusion.

In the social-political domain, I see no value more reliable and less tempting of abuse than the dignity of the human individual. In contrast, experience has convinced me that representatives of collective interest or transindividual norms are under strong temptation to abuse their power, especially if that power is doubled by being paired with the authority of the state. Such abuse can take the form of disciplining the citizens in the name of the working class or the nation, or disciplining individuals in the name of the religious community.

217. As the number of actual believers is much lower than the number of nominal faithful, the humble priest refers to the actual flock while the priest lacking humility refers to the nominal flock. Priests are in a position to attract adults and minors to their services. It is forbidden to keep anyone from attending or to force anyone to attend.

We have no acceptable way of measuring which denomination's spokesmen come closer to divine truth. We can direct our devotion toward any community, we can encourage our children to do so as well, we can turn our devotion in any other direction, if the devotion exists, but we are not entitled to judge anyone in matters of faith.

Setting an example is the most we can do to attract others to our own convictions. Beyond that or without it, nothing is left but cunning and violence. If priests employ political instruments against other priests in order to discredit competitors or draw away their faithful, then they have transgressed the fundamental democratic rules of play. Priests who extend their own under-sized faith and truth by worldly power mongering engage in behavior I find ugly. By doffing my imaginary hat, I pay homage to those priests who trust in the truth of their faith and teaching, who approach their fellow humans with humility.

September 1993

From Hate Talk to the Cattle Car

218. Historical facts exhibited in cattle cars. Those so inclined can imagine what it was like to ride the train for days with eighty others, into the unknown, to death in the gas chamber for the majority of the adults and invariably for children.

My schoolmates all took the train to Auschwitz. I managed to get to Budapest one day earlier, because my parents had already been taken away from the village we lived in.

My imagination can give me only a rough approximation of my schoolmates' experience in the cattle cars, on the selection ramp, and under the gas flowing from the shower. I state that these girls and boys were perfectly innocent, and that a crime comparable to their extermination has not occurred in the history of known horrors.

219. There have been murderous tyrannies; in our century, there have been concentration camps all over the globe, but the systematic slaughter of millions of children stands alone, unex-

---

On the fiftieth anniversary of the deportation of Jews living outside Budapest, a moving museum was created in cattle wagons of the type used to transport them.

plainable and irremediable. If we can speak at all of absolute crime, that was it.

We can conceive of the nature of this crime only if we imagine our own children or grandchildren facing the same plight. If we try to think of it for just a quarter of an hour, to see them in front of us as they would have been, we will start to get a feeling for this story.

220. Whose crime? It belongs to those who take it on themselves. The machinery of state that worked after the beginning of the German occupation was the same that worked before it, with the same armed men and officials. The same Parliament and the same leader empowered that machinery, which deported its own citizens beyond the national borders, knowing or not knowing what would become of them; at any rate, not making an effort to find out.

Perhaps they didn't have enough imagination. Perhaps, if they had known, if they had seen, if they themselves had experienced this thing, they wouldn't have done it. They did it because they did not see, because the speech of hatred blinded them, because the language of covert or overt anti-Semitism kept them from seeing the truth. A firm order and a few military countermeasures stopped the deportation of the Jews in the center of Budapest; deportation of Jews in the countryside could have been put off or avoided in the same way. If the administration had really not wanted it, the German commanders would not have been able to manage alone, without local cooperation. Local papers enthusiastically reported that their cities had become Jew-free.

221. Everyone who helped somebody escape or hide was a hero, a hero for behaving sanely, the way it is usual to behave with colleagues, friends, neighbors, the way Christian ethics demands. The way some priests and nuns acted. The sane counted

as exceptionally heroic, because the others suffered from blinding by words, ethical numbness, or a moral disease that can be compared to the great plagues, in a spiritual-intellectual sense.

222. Fascist speech marched through our region, and beside the great fascisms were little fascisms, half fascisms with their own death lists of various lengths. Sympathizers joined up for Hitler's Great Europe plan along the width and breadth of the continent, and for the most part they believed that this staggering plan could be accomplished only if they first freed themselves of their Jewish neighbors, if the Jews were taken somewhere, put where they belonged, as a public sanitation measure. The sympathizers believed it was possible and proper to form first verbal, then legal judgments on humans classified as members of a particular group or minority. The logic of such judgments, distinctions, laws, and decrees leads to the extermination of children.

Those who enjoy anti-Semitic speech should ask themselves whether they would enjoy watching a pile of children's corpses burning. Those who wouldn't enjoy seeing that shouldn't engage in anti-Semitic speech.

223. My schoolmates have already been smoothed into memories, just as the majority of survivors has; we become history irremediably, and those who demand from others more empathy than is offered should check their own capacity for it. If they do so, they might reach the conclusion that only relative punishment is possible for an absolute crime. That this story could have happened at all should make us shiver, not just for the victims but also for those who lived their own daily lives around it. The absolute crime was not committed by absolute criminals; most of the people who contributed work to the project believed they were doing their duty.

It didn't happen this way just in Central Europe; bureaucratic personnel in Western democracies were also disciplined collaborators in the deportation. For the most part. Not everyone. The Danes and the Bulgarians did not hand over their Jews. Why those countries in particular? There are those who hand over and those who don't. There are those who don't for a while, then suddenly do after all, if greater pressure is applied.

And once the decision was made, the train shipments were dispatched in a logistical tour de force, the rapid conveyance of living cargo beyond the national borders.

224. For the psychological explanation of this tour de force we do not need to look far: the culprit was not evil deep within the heart but, rather, language and the brutishness it caused. Really, can agreeing to the classification of children as garbage be anything but moral idiocy, spreading like an epidemic, making so many people on the Continent stupid? The Europe of which we are proud. The Europe that allowed the Jews to be killed. The Jews too were proud of Europe, and of their homeland(s) within it, even of their villages.

225. No infection similar to the one that struck the adult authorities, collaborators, malevolent supporters, and voluntary followers of the World War II era will be able to incapacitate so woefully future generations, provided that those generations regularly conduct themselves like the heroes among the Christian fellow citizens of the time, provided that not a single one of our citizens is allowed to be deprived of civil and human dignity first by word and then by deed.

Those who say that it's the Jews, the Hungarians, the Gypsies, the Romanians, the Catholics, the Greek Orthodox, the Muslim southern Slavs, and so on, since we could continue to list the names of peoples almost without end—those who say that their problem is a particular other people, those who are what they are by rejecting the other, those for whom this negative passion is the source of their patriotism are people who have already fallen ill.

They are already among the unfortunate, because they have caught the infectious disease that leads to sclerosis and paralysis of the imagination and morality.

226. I do not suggest that mad, blind people are not dangerous. There are such people today, although their number is not increasing dramatically, although within the four Visegrad countries the percentage of people expressing antipathy for Jews is lowest in Hungary, since only one of ten asked hates the Jews. But if that one in ten speaks high and low, as a tongue becomes habituated to rough language; if such speech grows roots; if open or discreet anti-Semitic speech appears to be a forgivable transgression, one that by being so common is no longer out of order; and if anti-Semitic rhetoric sneaks into political propaganda, then those who value their sight and their sanity should come to their senses and not tolerate it. Otherwise the language of rejection will become a possible and even profitable political maneuver.

My respect goes to all those who do not participate in the passionate parlor game of anti-Semitism. And my respect goes to all Jews who never collaborated in the rejection of minorities of any sort. My respect goes to all those who see the individual, not the abstract caricature, in others.

227. Allow me to summarize once more the point I am making. We cannot explain the infanticide of millions by the special evil of those who performed it and those who were responsible for it. Not criminals, but obedient officials and uniformed military personnel did what they did.

The explanation is not the deviant personality of the perpetrators but the political language of anti-Semitism, which built another kind of morality into their brains, that of ethnic purity, the ideal that leads to ethnic cleansing.

There are paths of thought that can be regarded as traps. If people start out along the path of anti-Jewish clichés, then from the analysis of the so-called Jewish question they will find them-selves step by step entering the group of active supporters of or retrospective apologists for the *Endlösung,* the final solution.

Political thinkers who would protect the majority from the mi-nority—or would remove a minority that endeavors to be law-abiding and patriotic and just wants to be left alone—will eventually reach some notion of final solution. Political paranoia will lead them there; it will take control of their reason. Those who imagine that they would be happier if another community did not exist will become spiritual-intellectual relatives of the child burners.

History sometimes grants monstrous success to some people or ideas. It is better not to think thoughts that could end in the deportation of any of our fellow humans, fellow citizens, fellow countrymen.

The Jews did learn one thing from the catastrophe of 1944. They should never again board a cattle car obediently.

1994

On the Ides of October

228. The morning of Sunday, October 15, 1944, was a bright one, with the sharp light of autumn. We were all abuzz from hearing the governor's cease-fire announcement. We lived in a Jewish house, above the Lloyd Cinema, packed together. Everyone in the house was Jewish, women, elderly people, children. The older men stood on a ladder to take down the yellow star painted on black cardboard over the entrance.

It suddenly occurred to us that we might stay alive, that we might go home, that we might see our parents, that everything would be as it was in the peace that perhaps had never even been.

We awaited confirmation of the news; the radio communicated nothing, however, only commands incomprehensible to us. The governor's proclamation was not followed by supporting speeches.

We walked around the block. Residents had not dared remove the distinguishing signs from the entrance of every house. One of the children set the yellow cardboard star on fire. We stood around it. A couple not wearing yellow stars walked by beside us arm in arm and the man in the hat said to the woman in the hat: "See, they've become insolent."

229. The new armed force did not appear anywhere; on the other hand, German military vehicles raced around the Körút, then came trucks full of men wearing green shirts and Arrow Cross ribbons. They wore expressions of excited determination. There were Jews who asked policemen what they should do now. Was there a new decree, could they stay out on the street after curfew? If I remember correctly, we were permitted to be in public only from eleven in the morning to five in the evening. It was disorderliness, even provocation, to loiter outside at five-fifteen in the afternoon.

Uncertainty was rife; no one knew what to do. What to do in case of a 180-degree turn, if official speech would no longer be of heroic struggle but, rather, of peace, if everything that had been would no longer be valid, and Jews would no longer be separated from the Aryan body of the nation. But what should we Jews do if it was no longer legal to hunt us down? We didn't know what we could do for ourselves.

230. By sunset, we had a hunch. The Arrow Cross chief announced the dismissal of the governor—we will fight beside our great German ally even more resolutely, for final victory, and we will cleanse our homeland, from me. Extermination is next, bedbug, cockroach, Jew—you're done for.

The intention was there; the rest was a question of coordination. The public annihilation of between one and two hundred thousand people might create a defeatist mood among the Christian population.

We thought a massacre was coming up, a night of long knives. Whoever was able to should hide, not stay at his address, disperse among Christian civilians, not stand out, melt into the environment, to avoid being picked out and taken around the corner to be shot.

From the corridor, we looked down at the movie screen, across the open roof. *I came from Tarnopol* was still showing, an anti-Semitic propaganda film. We rushed up and down the inner corridors of the building and dared to go out into the street, where we discussed the events excitedly.

We were quarry in the forest, and we feared the hunters, who were little people just like us, only a political development had put guns in their hands and given them verbal authority to kill even old people and children, those of the kind obligated by law to wear yellow stars.

231. The clumsy move of a clumsy governor: he lets the German ambassador know his intentions first and notifies his own troops only afterward! It was the kind of foolish loyalty that misled people here so many times and did not allow them to posit moral legality against the laws of dictatorship. I began from the premise that the legality that classified me "To be Exterminated" was unlawful, since I was innocent. I saw that in the image and name of our own state petty criminals could murder as easily as shooting a rabbit or catching a fly. The ultimate hostility emerged, the simple desire to take your life, and if no other method presented itself, it was prepared to shoot you and let you sink into the Danube.

232. I had an uncle Ödön, who was not the pride of the family, but he saved my life. When the Gestapo took my parents away, Uncle Ödön sent me a letter of invitation. His abandoning me later was a consequence only of his difficult situation; it does not erase his having saved us, my older sister Eva and me.

Not a good-looking man, he took pains to stand up straight, lifting his chin high and straining his shoulders backward. There was something affably condescending in his manners; he slapped my back to give me courage. Sometimes, however, he had surprising outbursts of emotion, which were utterly without charm.

In his company I constantly felt the close prospect of spiritual roughness. He wished to appear emphatically a gentleman, eating corn on the cob and peaches with a fork and knife.

In the 1920s Uncle Ödön swindled Grandfather out of his fortune; he sent Aunt Hermina, my mother's older sister, twenty-one red roses, to win the dowry he would use to straighten out his affairs. After the nuptials he first chided then went down on his knees to beg Grandfather to place his money in Ödön's bank. What will the son-in-law look like if even his father-in-law doesn't have confidence in the institution? Grandfather consented and transferred his money. The next day, Ödön's bank declared bankruptcy. My grandfather was ruined by the good offices of his son-in-law.

Ödön rented an apartment on Hollán Utca in Budapest, with help from the family. He opened a glove factory a block away, in a *sous-sol* with a white iron railing on its windows. The glove factory did tolerably well; they made a bourgeois living from it. Uncle Ödön straightened out.

While the anti-Jewish laws multiplied, his officer's medals of merit from World War I gave him an exemption, and in the summer of 1944 he still trusted that this exemption would last. The signum laudis and the iron crosses were there among the bric-a-brac and figurines in the vitrine.

Uncle Ödön had a special badge that allowed him to frequent the Jewish Council office. At home, he was the air-raid warden for the building. With his beeping lamp he marched up and down between the shelter and the ground floor, donning a shiny helmet under which his jaw jutted arrogantly, along with his rosy double chin. He visited the Jewish Council office daily, but he did not tell us what he did there.

233. We had to leave Uncle Ödön's apartment; the Jews had to squeeze together a little tighter. Uncle Ödön, Aunt Hermina, and

our two cousins got a little room with just enough space for the four of them to sleep. I remember a kind of heavy smell, friendly but unfamiliar elderly ladies, and children.

It was clear that there was no longer room for us here. Aunt Zsófi lived in the house next door; she wasn't even our relative, but the wife of my father's cousin, Dr. Gyula Zádor. My two cousins, István and Pál Zádor, already lived there, and Aunt Zsófi also had a son, Peter, who was close to our age. Others lived in this apartment as well. The face of a man with short-cropped, graying hair comes up from the fog of memory, along with an older kid and a bit of jumping around in the corridor. Aunt Zsófi was willing to take us in if Uncle Ödön fed us. For a few days we still went back to have lunch with our relatives.

234. On that night, October 15, Aunt Zsófi also went to hide with the boys, Peter, István, and Páli. With only a few bags, they went over to Margit Körut, to an apartment that an acquaintance had offered. They went up the stairs not wearing yellow stars. Shortly after they put down their bags, a resident of the house phoned to tell them to leave right away, because the concierge had reported them as possible Jews. Aunt Zsófi and the three boys dashed down the stairs at breakneck speed. They saw the elevator going up; inside were men of the Arrow Cross brigades, armed. The men banged on the door upstairs, but Aunt Zsófi and her charges were already at the bottom, scurrying back to the usual place of fear.

235. We also made ourselves scarce, "went into hiding," according to the expression of the time. We utilized Uncle Ödön's strategy, conveyed to us with grim arrogance. We escaped to the workshop called the glove factory, three blocks away. We couldn't take much with us, we didn't want to stand out, because the Arrow Cross brigades were already on patrol, though they hadn't gone into action yet. But we had to take something, after all, so that we could sleep on the cutting table, wash up in the

back, at the basin in the lavatory. We weren't allowed to turn on the lights in the *sous-sol*, but if the sun was shining outside, around noon there was enough light to read.

236. I was somewhat skeptical, not particularly inclined to return to the supervision of Uncle Ödön, because recently, sleeping in a room with my cousins from Berettyóújfalu, I had begun to feel more at home at Aunt Zsófi's. There, we were a natural *we* again, which meant the other branch of the family, my father's side, the branch of Páli and István's uncle on their father's side, Dr. Gyula Zádor, the neurologist presently engaged in forced labor, the portrait of irony in my childhood mythology. Every time I saw him, his amiable smile had a little inner merriment that imbued it with another, cooler light. It was a suspicious smile, as if he were making fun of me.

237. Because, for example, when I was five, I screamed in full passion on my hospital bed—Take this bandage off me! I've just woken from the anesthesia, I won't tolerate their tying me down, and I don't hear that I must stay calm in the immediate aftermath of an operation. The lack of trust also enrages me, as if I didn't have enough sense in my five-year-old body to stay quiet without being strapped down so humiliatingly. If those are the doctor's orders, I overrule them with sober reason. But since I come from the depth of unconsciousness, many around my hospital bed are delighted by my having returned to them, my mother most of all; only good radiates from her, I could be certain of her. It is self-evident: mothers should be where little boys are.

The white gauze with which they strapped me down on the white bed, and the white personnel in the white room, naturally induced antipathy on account of my preference for color. You are not so white, my angels, as you appear to be. My nanny Livia's housecoat is a warm beige, as it is of camel hair, and if she is domineering with me—for example, if she makes me swallow my syrup or holds my left arm down while taking my temperature—her aggression is accompanied with much physical kindness. But this unfamiliar middle-aged female is not entitled to handle my body just because she is wrapped in white. She can go to hell with her aggressive cheerfulness! I can see she's in a hurry, she would like to adjust a bandage. I'm bawling, and struggling a little too, which may have some connection to the bandage's having worked loose, and as I arch my back and scream to express my disgruntlement and that I won't, I won't stand for this, they better remove my straps, a familiar face appears at the foot of the bed: thick gray hair, a high forehead, and that insolent smile around the mouth, as if he doesn't believe my anger, as if he supposes I'm playing. Which of course isn't completely untrue. But what gives this white-robed figure the right to see into me? I didn't authorize him to do that, even if it was Uncle Gyula who had put on this white mask.

238. We hid from our own Doctor Spernáth behind the dining room curtain, so he wouldn't be able to stick us, so we wouldn't have to swallow the disgusting cod liver oil, and just for the sake of hiding, so we could soon give ourselves up to the complicity of giggles held back. Spernáth *bácsi* came to us in civilian clothes, in a gray suit, to talk politics with my father, listening to our chests in the meantime, a tickly and not really pleasant feeling, because Doctor Spernáth was bald and his cold pate had a kind of medicinal smell, which didn't have a good effect on us. We shivered when that head pressed against our naked chests.

239. Though Uncle Gyula wore a white robe, he nevertheless suggested that my straps be loosened, and suggested to me that I shouldn't fidget. The contract was made and kept.

240. Almost thirty years later, I asked another "ironist," psychologist Ferenc Mérei, about my uncle, whether they had

known each other, and he said something to the effect that my
uncle was considered half crazy.

In 1942, Dr. Gyula Zádor rents a big apartment downtown, at
Szép Utca 5, and furnishes it according to his wife's Bauhaus
taste. With his professional accreditation from Heidelberg and
his position as chief neurologist of the Jewish Hospital, he opens
his private practice.

He does this as if there were no World War II and Third
Reich, he does this because it is the thing to do according to
bourgeois logic. He finds a beautiful woman and wins her from
her husband, a successful journalist. Zsófi has interesting connections, poets, painters, all kinds of revolutionaries.

Uncle Gyula's background is more modest and respectable, the
family in Berettyóújfalu, which now gives him his portion of the
estate so he can get started. The Berettyóújfalu branch of the family builds a house, which is a store or factory at the same time. My
uncle and aunt are their own bosses, and they like to go across and
visit at the warm family bay whenever it suits them. In the workshop or store, we see the street, the world. The back rooms and the
kitchen are the Beidermeier zone, the world of passions, with frequent alternation of happiness and despair, the malaria of being ef-
fusive and taking offense. There in the back the whole world is
gorgeous, then the next moment the whole world is horrible.

So this global citizen from Berettyóújfalu, who dared to look
ironically at us born-and-bred Újfalusi-ites, settles down nicely
here in the capital, as if we were living through normal times, as
if everything were proceeding entirely in order, as if the highest
priority for him now was to build up his clientele and to publish
further articles in the domestic and international professional
literature.

241. In the yard, down there in the gazebo, he sat in pants
pressed mirror-smooth, yellow shoes, and a bluish-pink silk shirt,
quite a swank image. In conversation he was a good listener,

allowing us villagers to turn our fine phrases, but he was also a city slicker, with his own inner half-smile about everything.

We identified naively with ourselves, not knowing much about irony or the fact that existence is dual and that love too can be malicious. Uncle Gyula gave his village optimism a twist with a little of the urban ability to see behind things. The city person bumps his nose into everything and always knows what's behind things. As if the truth of things is always somewhere else rather than in the way it is presented.

If your eyes see well, you can tell from straight ahead what others can find out only by peeping. It's not necessary to go through all those contortions.

When Uncle Gyula looked at me that way, he wasn't yet forty years old. Now that I'm sixty, I feel that the naive part of Uncle Gyula's soul would have come to be dominant had he lived. Perhaps it became dominant even as things were, to his undoing; he acted the part of the law-abiding villager.

242. He could have escaped from his forced labor camp; they even gave him leave for a day to see his family, on Christmas of 1944. Despite his wife's remonstrations, the doctor went back, because he had promised his commanding officer and also owed it to his patients. In the meantime, the sympathetic commander was fired, and reliable Doctor Zádor, along with his patients, poets, and essayists, was shot and thrown into a mass grave.

243. Aunt Zsófi must have been thirty then. Sometimes a malicious light would appear in her eye, and her voice had a kind of fineness that came from another shore. She was an autonomous person. While her husband was in a forced labor camp, she lived in half of a three-bedroom apartment with her son and her husband's two cousins.

And then what happens? She gets two more children from

Berettyóújfalu. She didn't ask for them, but she gets them. By the kindness of fate and Uncle Ödön.

She didn't hesitate to do as her taste dictated, to treat them as her own, to recognize that she now had five children. She didn't share her strategic reflections with us—it was clear she did what she could—but she also made an effort for human dignity not to be diminished by the inglorious circumstances, for the children to be able to live through this abominable time with their souls intact.

244. But for now we still hide in the glove factory; for now we sleep on a chair the night of October 15. No rumble of gunfire comes from outside; we could think the worst is over. In the dark factory, we suddenly start to miss the comforts of home. Especially Uncle Ödön—in the morning he discovers that the shaving brush from his shaving kit has been left at the apartment. It is painfully missed. Though a bit of foam can be conjured with one's fingers after wetting and soaping, and the razor works even if one's skin has been softened without foam, the beauty is lost, and neither the operation nor the result will be satisfactory.

Even if last night wasn't the night of long knives, it is still not advisable to go home, but the shaving brush really ought to be retrieved. I admit, there would have been something comical about Uncle Ödön's stepping from his hideout, going to his home three blocks away, then coming back and carefully locking the front door with its iron grate. If he goes back for the brush, then why doesn't the whole family go home and wait to see what will happen, or perhaps to inquire about a better hiding place?

Shaving without a brush and going unshaven were both miserable options. The most reasonable solution, in Uncle Ödön's view, was for me to go and get the brush.

245. I started on my way. At the third house from the glove factory, I hit a trap. Soldiers wearing armbands stood at the gate. It

was drizzling, and perhaps they didn't even know exactly what they were supposed to do. They called me over: "Hey junior, come over here. Aren't you a Jew?" "Why would I be?" I asked. "Well, you just might be," they said. "I might be," I said. "But you aren't?" "Why would I be?" I said, reverting to my original question. "Listen here, that's the way Jews talk." "Are you a Jew?" I asked. "Why would I be?" he asked. "Because you know so much about how they talk." "All right, pull your pants down!" I didn't move; we stared at each other. "Well, how about it?" "It's raining." "All right, get going." He knew and I knew what was up. That soldier didn't want to kill me.

From there to the apartment nothing of note happened. The older women interrogated me there about where the family spent the night. I no longer remember what I mumbled, something about a visit. They saw me take the brush from the shelf under the bathroom mirror and stick it into my pocket. "You came back for that?" one of the old ladies asked. "Well, goodbye now, ma'am," I said. She stuck a roll into my hand. I munched that on the way downstairs.

246. On the corner, I saw that the Arrow Cross men were running in my direction on Hollán Utca, so I took a quick left and tried to get back to the family via a little detour on Pozsonyi Utca.

I hadn't counted on the Arrow Cross men running parallel to me, however, or on there being a lot of them, a solid line spanning the entire width of Pozsonyi Utca, and from behind, on Szent István Körút, another squad approached, so that they could completely hem in the people on the street. Around that time, it wasn't hard to find Jews at noon in the Újlipótváros district.

What did they do to those they picked out? Maybe they took them to the brick factory in Obuda; from there the captives could be marched westward and possibly put onto freights. A few more weeks had to pass before the Arrow Cross men began to use the simplified procedure of shooting them on the bank of the Danube.

I didn't know what happened to those selected—for example, to the thin bespectacled man who wore a white armband and chattered about some kind of exceptional status, saying that he had risked his life during the time of the commune. The Arrow Cross man said nothing, then spit a cigarette butt in the man's face and pulled him aside.

The whole street was blocked. People stood in line in front of the ID checkers; papers weren't enough, there were questions to be answered.

I located a brigade member wearing a leather jacket and a leather cap with its brim folded up, examining people with his hands on his hips. There were two people ahead of me. I got down on all fours and crawled past his brown hunting boots. It was a fairly chaotic scene, so he couldn't keep track of what was going on underneath and beside him.

I was careful to walk home slowly, going around the block. I waited and watched until there was no one around before knocking on the door of the factory.

247. "So, you're back?" Uncle Ödön said, giving me a kindly pat on the head. He shaved, was generous with the cologne, then caressed his chin as he walked up and down. It was lunchtime. He said that this wasn't a good hiding place and that everyone should go back to where he had lived up to now. My older sister Éva and I should go back over to Uncle Ödön's apartment over the Lloyd Cinema for lunch, but only after four in the afternoon. We should wait for our late lunch over at "that woman's." He meant Aunt Zsófi; he liked to refer to her disapprovingly.

At four in the afternoon, however, when we rang the bell, the only one to open it was the elderly woman who had noticed my taking the shaving brush that morning. To my question—Where's the family?—she said that they left and didn't say where they were going. We went there the next day, and the day after that, but there was no news of our relatives. After that, we received lodging, rations, and care only from Aunt Zsófi.

I ran into Aunt Hermina in April 1945 in Nagyvárad. I saw her on a street corner and did a double take. She continued on her way, on the other side of the street. A week later, we ran into each other and stood face to face. My aunt suggested that I go with her, now. I demurred. She told me their address, so I could visit them. With an uncertain promise, I quickly said goodbye and went on my way.

1993

Remembering October

248. Fifty years ago today, I had to crawl across the raid lines of the Arrow Cross brigades to save my skin. In 1944, I learned that adults could unexpectedly go mad, that in uniform or not they could proceed to hunt down children and elderly people.

There were all kinds among the hunters. They worked in loose squadrons. What they had in common was that they had been authorized to hunt human beings. They were allowed to kill a person on the spot, to "execute on site," using the terminology of the time, for being a Jew or a deserter from the army.

249. Around Christmas, our building too had some of its residents escorted to the bank of the Danube, where they were lined up facing the water. A burst of gunfire, and they were knocked over like bowling pins and fell among the drifting ice floes.

The people who did this killing came to the apartment where eighty of us were hiding anxiously. They weren't machines; they were people similar to us but who happened to view the world differently. They demanded money and engagement or wedding rings and in the interests of national security they collected the kitchen knives.

We had to line up in front of the building. We children had decided that if they led us in the direction of the Danube, we would scatter; they couldn't get all of us, one of us might escape. Then two people in officers' uniforms came, scolded the militiamen, and ordered us back into the building.

Then the Arrow Cross brigades came again, and one of them took a few adults away to be shot. The children they left alone. Then a tall, good-looking young man shot an old man in the head, in the doorway of the building, right next to me. He trained his pistol on me next. We looked at each other; he let his hand down, turned, and left.

250. These militiamen with armbands had to decide. It was left to them to shoot or not to shoot. They didn't need to give cause or justification for their decision before the law. There was no law, only their souls, their spirits.

I must say, they were unprepared, almost like children left alone; they hesitated. Because they had learned *Thou shall not kill,* but also that certain kinds of people should be killed and were easily killed. Anyone the chief points to, you can shoot. In their hearts there was a chief who pointed at this one or that. I could say that those days are long over and that sane civilian men are no longer capable of such acts. Yet daily we see that south of us, a few hundred kilometers away, sane civilian men speaking the same language kill a person casually, from time to time, for being Catholic, Greek Orthodox, or Muslim.

Their ancestors converted or were commanded to convert by someone to their present creeds, and now, because one prays this way and the other prays another way, to the same God, or doesn't even pray, as the case may be—in other words, because of something that before did not impede them at all in joint work, friendship, and marriage—now, suddenly inflamed by angry and small-minded people, they kill with little restraint.

Some of them enjoy being snipers, flattening standing figures with a finger movement.

251. What do their priests tell these young men? What does the opinion-making intelligentsia encourage them to do? Learned people in high positions tell them: You cannot live together, you must separate. This said to people who got along quite well together. The civil war was not started by plain folks. This spirit of baseless, bull-headed hatred—from now on we cannot bear each other—sometimes gets a grip on spouses, friends, parents, and even children. Because there's a time for opening and a time for closing.

We can decide, however, to work for understanding, by word, deed, or art. We may choose to protect human beings rather than to hunt human beings.

People with whom we live under one roof are the ones who require from us the most protection. And we need to fear not only those beyond the door. Protecting humanity, primarily against itself, is always timely.

Fifty years ago, there were also protectors of humanity, who took orders from their own consciences. I too was saved by them; I have grounds to believe that if anyone deserves to be called heroes, they do.

252. If Carl Lutz, secretary of the Swiss Embassy and a worthy colleague of the Swede Raoul Wallenberg, acting with brave Jewish coworkers, hadn't given out thousands of letters of protection in Budapest at the end of 1944, testifying that the undersigned were under the protection of the Helvetian Confederation, and if a recalcitrant Swiss public official (the ambassador was unwilling to sign these letters of protection), hadn't allowed his conscience to overrule the official regulations, then perhaps I and many others would not be able now to pay grateful respect to

the memory of Carl Lutz. I was one of those who survived the reign of the Arrow Cross in a Swiss protected house. The Arrow Cross brigades haphazardly took a few people from the house out to the Danube, but the majority of the Jews in it stayed alive.

253. From this story of the Swiss collective emigration passport, of the great mass of Swiss *Schutzpassen*, it is evident that individual feelings can make a difference even in the most ominous situations. Lutz was not ordered to save people; he gave himself the order.

And when he delivered a reminder to the Arrow Cross government, referring to President Roosevelt in setting forth the prospect of personal responsibility for those implicated in further barbarism, the momentum of systematic deportation and arrests followed by summary executions ebbed, because the guilty trembled.

It is possible to do something even against terror. One can save a handful or even thousands of people. If the resistance is forceful, the commanders of terror become uncertain, and at least some victims can escape. There are few situations perfectly closed and hopeless.

254. A few courageous and conscientious Jews carried out the messenger work for Carl Lutz. Most of them were Zionists who rejected the role of resigned victim on philosophical grounds. If protectors of humanity give up, evil and indifference will harden into implacable destiny. The rescue was possible because there were people who made the attempt, people who found Carl Lutz, and accepted the risks of action, knowing that if they didn't try, rescue would surely be impossible.

In the self-defense of Jews, Zionists were the most successful, usually through the distribution of half-official, half-false papers. Had the generation of Hungarian Jewry, which was then in adulthood, not trusted loyally, out of respect for the law, had they not shut their eyes to the gradually advancing design of the final solution, to the machinery of European Jewry's annihilation, then at least the gaps through which escape was possible would have been wider, then those who had false papers pressed into their hands would have tried to use them, then the great majority of Hungarian Jews would not have rejected the path that appeared to be unlawful, a rejection driven by cowardice in some cases certainly, but brave men too rejected unlawfulness, out of their loyalty to the state.

This sentiment was evident in the appeals of the Jewish Council as well: Let us be obedient, law-respecting citizens. They sprinkled hope that the reward for obeying would be more dignified treatment. The authorities rewarded this obedience with more expeditious death.

In our chasing of illusions we imagined *Waldsee* as a lake surrounded by woods. We heard that they were taking us there and we didn't know it was the cover name for Auschwitz. We would have been able to learn its real name and what it meant, if our parents and grandparents hadn't shut their eyes, not wanting to believe the increasingly grim evidence.

255. A half-century later, within the general history of the annihilation of European Jewry, remembrances of the gradients in the annihilation of Hungarian Jewry occur one after another. It happened in steps, and as long as it affected only foreign citizens, as long as it concerned only those living in the countryside, as long as it affected only those Jews living on the perimeter of the city, there was always hope, always some way to explain why it was they and why it wouldn't be we.

When we recall this design, with its many chapters and increasingly ruthless advance, to which Jews living in the various countries could not respond with adequate clear-sightedness and resoluteness, we are justified in examining the psychological and moral causes of helplessness.

The armed and civilian administration of deportation did not spring up from nowhere, it did not emerge from the netherworld. Had the Jews' vision been sharper, they would have seen what was happening. Those among them who did something, did so because they knew what was happening.

256. One must not accept the role of victim. Those who have children cannot be resigned. The victim's role is a bad one, because it surrenders responsibility. The victim decides nothing, only obeys. But man's fate designated him for decision, to decide what is good and what is bad, every day of his life. Those who were not completely immured in resignation were able to do something for themselves and had a better chance of escaping.

257. The Jews can be exterminated if the mood of the world is such that peoples can be exterminated. And if the Jews can be exterminated, then the next people classified as unnecessary will follow in turn. Then there will be no fellow men, only categories, rubrics, numbers.

258. The only ones who can help others are those who have enough strength of spirit and sovereignty to help themselves, and to defend themselves, to defend whatever about them is being attacked.

If the protection of human beings is not the dominant idea, then the world's righteous people, those further ahead on the path of moral understanding, can save only a few here and there. Even if they are not saints, they are heroes. We are, after all, imperfect. We are all changeful and anxious souls; that is our frailness and our greatness; we are not machines.

Those who were saved are obligated both to those who were

killed and to the rescuers. I find deep the Talmudic saying that if someone saves one person, he saves the world. Such a person opens a gate to hope and a window to the light. Such a person gives proof that there are fellow men in whom one can trust, and that there are handshakes that hold true.

1994

In Bihar

259. By February 1945 my older sister Éva and I had found our way back to the village from which our parents were taken, the village we left on the last day before the deportation. Had we stayed until the next day, we would have been taken to Auschwitz. My fourteen-year-old sister might have survived. I was eleven; Doctor Mengele sent all my classmates to the left, that is, into the gas chamber. He left alive only the twelve-year-old Franfurt boys, who were twins; he experimented on them.

260. I was cold a lot of the time then, in the early spring of 1945 in Berettyóújfalu. It got dark early, so I read by candlelight in the unheated big room. A petroleum lamp burned in the kitchen. The woman of the house, the fat wife of a coachman, peeled potatoes, sorted peas, and sat near the stove. Her son was over three. He said, "Mother dear, I'm hungry," whereupon the woman of the house let out her huge gelatinous breast. The child stood and suckled. Either he stood on the stool or his mother leaned forward a little. The room smelled a little of the stove, of bed. I rested my elbows on the windowpane. It got dark early. I don't remember what I read. My sister Éva did more sitting in the kitchen, I did more wandering about.

Nothing was real; here we were in Berettyóúfalu, and yet we weren't home. Uncle Imre Székely, my father's second cousin, supported us. He was a warm-hearted, mumbling, quiet man, broad-shouldered, funny, straightforward. He waited in vain for his wife, Aunt Lenke; his daughter, Panni; and his son, Gyuri, to come back from Auschwitz. I thought less often of my parents returning while I was there. Uncle Imre could not hope anymore; at night, he would moan in anguish. I still hoped. I knew my parents had been taken to Austria, and the war was still going on there.

It was the same and yet not the same. I sat there in school and felt a kind of chilliness. It was not possible to discuss the previous year with my classmates. No one had wanted to kill them. And the Arrow Cross brigades had wanted to kill me in the name of my classmates, at least that's the sort of thing the brigades said. My classmates in the second grade of public school were not made questionable for being what they were. I was the only Jewish boy in class; they were a little afraid of me. Ahead of me, and behind me, was great uncertainty.

Every day, I would walk past the rolled-down blinds of my father's hardware store. Anyone could have gone up to the apartment by the side entrance; they could have rummaged through the garbage, but they would have found nothing of value. Sometimes I went into the yard and up the stairway to the second floor, then walked through the empty rooms and looked down at the carriages driving past on the main street. A couple sat straight-backed on a coach, both of them wearing fur caps. There was some rustling behind me, Gypsy kids spying to see what I was looking for, or if I had found anything, because if so, I could lead them to something too.

261. I don't remember how, but we found out that we would soon be going to Nagyvárad in a Russian truck, because an uncle of mine who lived in Bucharest was coming to meet us in

"Várad" and take us in. For money, the soldiers were willing to transport us over the border. It wasn't even a real border yet; in the fall, Nagyvárad and Berettyóúfalu were still in one country, even one county. Now they were separate. In the spring, neither Bucharest nor Budapest gave the orders here, only the Russians did, along with the local authorities that always sprang up from somewhere. We weren't really asked if we wanted to go; my father's friends made the decision; it was clear that we would go where someone could take us in permanently.

March was morose: muddy, gray, cold. We had learned how to tell if we were in the way, but we had also learned how to find it natural enough to be wherever we were, and for someone to feed us. We grew quiet, we couldn't daydream, though we were only a stone's throw from our house. Up until now, we had longed to be here, we figured we would be the grown-ups. Once we arrived, the daydream crumbled, we were children.

The wind blew around old family letters in my room, and the pages of the prayer book in the temple. We could feel our weakness; we wouldn't be able to clean out this much garbage, we wouldn't be able to start a new life. Where we lived, the room was cold, the kitchen noisy. There was no library in the village.

262. As I had done in my father's store, I loitered in the sparsely stocked little shops run by Jews who had returned from forced labor. Two or three of them would get together, one of them would buy, the other would sell; they had become friends after being deported together; they were on equal terms for having lost their families, they could do nothing else. Brown sugar, flannel, and hoes were still available for money, later only in exchange for eggs, then for flour, but the door kept opening, customers came.

Widowed young men looked at women again, and women began to trickle home from the forced labor camps. There were local Christian women, formerly typists, nannies, maids. Or, if a wife had been killed, perhaps her little sister had survived. A woman entered the house, the bed, and by the end of the year, by the next spring, children were born. The loss of the original family was no longer a nightmare, but an abrasive reality. If everything worked out, one could mourn one's dead beside the new wife and the new child, with silence rather than with speech.

263. Several people escorted us to the grayish-green truck, a Studebaker, if I remember correctly. It was covered by canvas, and since there were benches inside, it served to transport people. There were packages on board too, so many that there was no place to put my legs; the black market was brisk. Beside the chauffeur sat a master sergeant who learned the language of every country as the Soviet troops advanced and who quickly found his legs in local commerce. He sold me a Cossack cap and traded me a sword for an alarm clock. Later, he came into the dormitory in Debrecen to ask if I wanted to ride home in their jeep for a little leave in "Újfalu." The overloaded jeep raced; my legs hung out. I still enjoy thinking of that grinning master sergeant. I peeked out from under the canvas; the sun shone, the meadow was green.

264. In Nagyvárad, someone escorted the two of us, my sister and I, to an address. Chubby women lived there, their attention fully occupied by caring for an infant; my sister was happy to join them in that. I received an apartment one floor higher and gave myself over to a comfortable loneliness. The apartment belonged to someone who had returned from forced labor; he used to be a lawyer, now he would be a prosecutor. He traveled on official business. He too had lost his family. He didn't sleep at home, so I could use his apartment; I could sit out on his balcony overlooking the Körös River. There were bottles of liquor in one of the cabinets, and I consumed them one by one.

It was the first time I had the opportunity to wake up in an apartment where the spring sun shone in, or spend hours on the balcony with a book in my hands and muse on the completeness of the moment, on my good fortune, which appeared to be staying, and which I wanted no external disturbance or distraction to interfere with. There is an inspired state in childhood, when we know even what we don't "know" officially, though we have no particular need for the knowledge, since being here now is joy enough, perhaps walking along the riverbank in the April sunshine, or by shop windows on Main Street, or under the arcades of Canon's Row, feeling a faint springlike hope that I would see my parents again.

265. My father's house, my aunt's house, perhaps this is it. I go by smell, I look for a chest of drawers or a walnut tree, I look for a dining room cabinet covered by a lace cloth, I look for the porcelain figures in the glass case that can be broken by a rifle butt.

The interiors of yards remind me of dinners past, under the trellis. The good life requires not only material comfort but also ease and, most of all, staying alive. Consommé, coffee, and cigars all need to be given their due.

This was a life in which everything had a place and time. Like ironed shirts set one upon the other in nice columns, the tasks to be completed took their place one upon the other: the time for opening letters and writing, the time for cards and history books, the time for the *Neue Züricher Zeitung* and the *Pester Lloyd*, the Budapest and provincial papers, the pro-government and opposition papers. The time for napping and the time for going to the café, the time for walking and the time for the theater. This was a life in which grandfathers had no reason not to hang their jackets always on the same peg when they changed into a tobacco-colored housecoat over their vests.

266. At the end of the 1930s, when I started being able to follow the grown-ups' conversations, there was plenty to talk about around the table. Rebellious sons travelled not to Vienna or Ab-

bazia but to Paris or London. They did not travel to Moscow. They left Berlin. They made impatient declarations at the table.

Using the silver dining service, they ate the food brought in by the maid (in more modest homes, by the cook) after someone pushed a button built into the table (in more modest homes, hung above the table), the button which made a bell ring in the kitchen, telling the maid to come in, take away the dirty plates, and bring the next course.

Quiet permanence seemed to prevail in the weekly menu and in the starched bonnet worn above the forehead by the help. Even if the faces and names changed, from Juliska to Piroska, from Erzsi to Irma, from Regina to Vilma, the way meals were prepared and served was not much altered.

The young people could not explain sensibly what was intolerable about the whole thing, since everyone was satisfied, from Juliska to Vilma. They found good husbands, had dowries, so it was difficult to define the strange relationships they were imposing not just on themselves but on everyone else too. They talked a lot of nonsense, and one or another dependent heir went so far as to speak out passionately in favor of free love.

267. I stood on the balcony in a coat, watching the Körös as the foam pushed onto the rocks, as the river grumbled and resounded. There was a brisk current, if not a flood.

My hair grew long, I avoided the barber, I saw the film *Six Hours after the War* three times in the cinema. I observed the internees, and among them the unforgettable soccer star: they marched away to clean up the rubble every day, escorted by a policeman in a mix-and-match uniform. Only an old rifle lay on the policeman's shoulder; his charges could have escaped, but they marched on, one, two, one.

Once I had completed the required interlude on the warm second floor, around the baby, among the fat ladies, I went up to my own apartment, where there were a few books. I looked out at the Körös, and I was happy to have an empty apartment behind me.

Sometimes I could spend hours watching the river pounding the rocks. I used opera glasses to watch the fish jumping, the bushes on the shore, and the iron fence. I closed my eyes and tried to listen to just the water. I hung on to the chair's armrest and rocked my head back and forth until I was dizzy. I wanted not to think about anything.

268. A month passed easily, though it did have blacker patches. One was the receiving office for people who had returned from deportation; I went there in the mornings. At the end of April and the beginning of May, there were already some people from liberated camps.

The women and men in striped suits came, most of them only half in stripes, dressed eclectically, one could say. They were thin. Their faces had regained some color, but their voices came from the depth of wells, they spoke through thick rock, and their glances swept around—where would the blow come from?

The deported, clients, gathered in a big hall. On the basis of some sort of registry, the officials behind the windows gave news of who was alive and who wasn't. They also gave out civilian clothing. Many people left carrying their striped clothes in their hands; others left their camp clothes at the office, they didn't want to remember.

I asked the not very friendly woman sitting behind the window if she knew anything about my parents. She didn't. I left her our address. I sat down in a chair in the hall and waited for them to come, because here they would get civilian clothing for their stripes and perhaps a little money and news about where we were. How could they go anywhere else but to where we were? My mother was from Nagyvárad, she would naturally return to Nagyvárad, all people would return to their place of birth, from where their family traveled to the gas chamber—her older sisters, her children, and her grandchildren. Maybe someone would come back, even if the children didn't, because there was no possibility that the children would come back. I tried to imagine my parents stepping in, going to the window. I would let them get as far as asking about us before I sneaked up behind them and touched them.

269. I wondered if they had changed a lot. Would it be easy for us to recognize one another? The returnees showed pictures, all depicting people who gazed at the world with even-tempered innocence. But in contrast the returnees themselves had become lined; this year had engraved the knowledge of death and mourning upon them, even upon the most vulgar of them.

There were some who sat beside me and tried to be encouraging: if my parents had been taken not to Auschwitz but to Austria, then their chances of survival were better, but one still couldn't know anything definite, battles were still going on there. I had to hope that my parents were still alive under German rule, in other words, in constant danger of death, because it would have been worse to imagine that they had been taken to Auschwitz. What happened there, I had already heard.

270. In the room where I sat, I was the only child. No Jewish children had survived from Nagyvárad and its environs. I asked about the gas chamber. We sat on the bench, and the women told me that the Polish-Jewish prisoners took their children away from them and pushed the little ones toward a grandmother or another old woman. The prisoners wanted to save the women, so they wouldn't have to escort their children into the gas chamber on the basis of a wave by Doctor Mengele.

The doctor must have been especially angry at the children; he sentenced even younger women, still capable of working, to death by gas if they held a child's hand. The child must die immediately and unconditionally. Children and everyone with whom they were in physical contact the doctor waved to the left, as a person slaps his palms together when a mosquito hovers on the porch in the summer. In my peers he saw not children but pests. He saw the children's faces, and he didn't see them; his eyes were covered by cataracts made of words. A military officer, arrogant, smart, carrying out orders unconditionally. If the assignment was to destroy Jews down to the very last one, then there is no room for individual discretion, then all these Jewish children were just bits of the mass to be liquidated. Then it didn't matter what they were like, it only mattered that they were Jews. They said the doctor was a good-looking, vain young man, nothing special. Probably he was interested more in his scientific career than in these anthropomorphic experimental animals. Among them, he needed the twins, since the Führer would be pleased if someone discovered a way to help Aryan or even just German mothers multiply, while keeping others from multiplying. In time the fecund Germans would fill all of Europe. Their numbers would be increased by orders of magnitude if patriotic German women systematically bore twins.

271. I was one of a kind as I sat there. Some parents didn't even look at me, some looked at me and cried, and some wanted to give me things, which I didn't accept. There was a woman who shook me and cried too. This was too much for me, my address was there, they would find me if they wanted to, if they came. I didn't go back to the receiving office for the deported.

October 1993

Longing in the Desert

272. Ten o'clock at night, Bersheva, a room in a third- rather than second-class hotel, called the Desert Inn. If I consider how few things of any kind are here, this hotel room is great, just for existing, though the telephone doesn't work, and the air-conditioning is noisy rather than effective.

I've just come from Ben Gurion University, where a tenth of Israel's teachers and students work, with one-fifth of the financial support from American and other Jews. They gave out honorary doctorates, and it was clear that the university is a national labor of love for the locals and for wealthy donors whose names are borne by institutes and departments. Everyone wants to immortalize himself, the scholar and the university president, the rabbi and the rich man, and all proudly profess themselves members of one concern, one family.

The whole day passed in a strange duality. Combined with a guided tour. It is a job that the chauffeur-guide has learned, it's his profession, he's a good patriot, well indoctrinated. Everyone is. You can only be *we*. Sad smiles and hope. There is historical hope. Ben Gurion's vision connecting a homeland and books. The visionary died after his wife, among bookshelves filled with

Spinoza and Jewish scholarship, Plato and Buddhism, in a small one-story house, modest even for workers' quarters in Europe.

They show me around, I see the sites of the great research projects—how can the desert be turned green?—I see a little oasis, then just desert weeds and the Bedouins' tents. I try to imagine the desert made fertile. There is water, the Bedouins' sheep drink. There are trees, too, around the institute.

For those who are here, this is very good. Everything is very good for those who are in it.

The chauffeur rails against Foreign Minister Peres: to give only, to give always? And what do they (the Arabs) give?

If my memory serves, I was never as alone as I am here. Why should I force myself to be especially *we,* with these people above all others? I spoke to many kind people, but their consciousness is insular, they cannot exist in any other way.

273. Peace, peace, everyone speaks of peace. But we ourselves are always the greatest threat to peace. Ideological and religious-ethnic triumphalism, paranoia, and suprematism. If the Jews cannot perceive the Arabs as equal to them, if they do not make peace with the Arabs within themselves, if they demand reciprocity always, in every detail, then there will not be peace.

The offenses cannot be undone. Everyone remembers his wounds. Understanding the other is peace. But how can one who is uncertain of himself understand the other? And which of the concerned parties is not uncertain of himself? Because of the extremes on the other side, the dignified middle of the road always convulses.

European Jews learned the cultures of the European peoples, but Israeli Jews have not learned to speak Arabic. There will not be peace, just an effort at peace; but there is also truth to the statement that there is no alternative to peace. Peace will not come from more war, more victory, and more humiliation. The desire for revenge exists on both sides. It is worthwhile for the

Palestinians to organize themselves into a state, because then there will be legitimate and realistic authority above them.

Let there be a state, so that the Palestinian elite will behave responsibly and understand the law of mutual dependency.

Can friendship be built upon a feeling of superiority? What is peace other than trusting that we will support one another's interests? Knowing how the other can be hurt and avoiding such behavior. We are all sensitive, skeptical, vulnerable, with unstable self-respect both individually and as a group. When we assure one another that we are wonderful, we repress our worries. Jews and Arabs must become individuals for each other. The Arabs know Hebrew; why don't the Jews know Arabic?

Peace is not a cease-fire. Peace can be made only by the whole of society. Judaism must come to be on good terms with Islam, and individual Jews must come to be on good terms with individual Arabs. Israeli civilians cannot hide behind their soldiers. With a fair and honorable offer, Israeli citizens could make peace with Arab citizens.

Generosity is rewarded. It is possible to behave in such a way that politeness will not be construed as a sign of weakness.

In reality, neither party will subordinate its existence or desired sovereignty to the other, neither will give in to the other, both have pride and the hot temper of the Near East. Peace is quite a complicated structure; mutual recrimination and strict incommunication—the "we just don't talk to them" attitude—is a bad climate for it.

Peace is the only solution, but it requires much hard work and time, patience, and the avoidance of overreaction. The tumor of conflict is generally aggravated by petty gestures, for example, the seemingly insignificant expropriation of a plot of land. There are, of course, some who believe that even more land should have been expropriated, and that violence supported by legal rhetoric should be increased.

274. Humanity is childish. It has not degenerated from some height; rather, it is not mature. It is not there yet. In the Germans' case, there was a too rapid transition from the small state's perception of impotence to the consciousness of being a great power, from being little men to almost complete rule

Crime? The desire to dominate the other. Children wrestle too, every game is about who will end up on top. It is a fact that the Arabs were here in the Near East, and even if their flow into land of Palestine occurred more in the twentieth century, they didn't come from very far away. The Zionist Jews, however, came from Europe, the children of Jews from Russia, Poland, Germany, Austria, Hungary, Romania and so on. It is also a fact that they fled from extermination, either because they sensed that it would happen or because they survived it somehow.

275. The Jews and the Muslims are a challenge for each other. Naturally, the situation is the same with the Jews and the Christians, because the monotheisms can't get along together nicely, or blend subtly, though that would be more civilized conduct.

But to keep to the subject of Jews, they are incapable of believing in God identified as a person, just as they cannot accept a God identified as a plant, animal, or celestial body.

Allah has only one prophet, another exclusivity that the Jews just don't acknowledge. According to them, God has more than one designated interpreter, pluralism reigns, there are prophets and wise men, and this is as it should be. There are classical authors.

Even if I do not believe in the interfering, creative, personal God, who is here constantly and supervises me, I do feel something of the sort, sometimes, when I pray. At those times I need someone I can address, someone to ask for strength, someone I can think of as my better self, my father, my lord, superior to me and present, knower of my every heartbeat and of the truth, the eternal other, my better double.

This deliberately indeterminate notion does not require undue gullibility, it requires me only to recognize my own limitations and to suppose that God is that which is beyond them, beyond all of humanity's limitations.

"Maybe there is someone greater than I am, because I am rather small, even together with all of mankind," thinks a person in more humble moments.

276. The technological-moral success of the Jews humiliated the Arabs. But the Arabs can be confident in themselves, because they are many. Will there be, can there be genuine dialogue with Iran and Iraq, can fundamentalisms negotiate? If they do not recognize each other's right to exist, it will be difficult.

Fundamentalisms stretch a partial truth and call it the whole truth. They subordinate to some idea an individual's will to survive.

If they want to live, citizens adjust, passively for the most part; they are scared, and only those who do not know fear should condemn that. "Why weren't you a hero? Why weren't you a martyr?" the strict ones ask.

277. The responsibility of the intelligentsia becomes more substantial on both the Jewish and the Arab side. The mission of the intelligentsia is actively to make peace. To open communication with others, about whom we know either nothing or something unfavorable. The mission of the intelligentsia is self-criticism in the first person plural. For this they are often despised. Excommunicated. Bypassed. The others rage and crow with a community, and the Jews do the same.

There is no developed Jewish self-criticism. Where it does begin to emerge, one or another author gives up his Judaism and converts to the Christian or the Muslim faith. The self-critic becomes a self-denier. This is not the way of the Bedouin tribal chief. The head of the family sits with his four wives. They are well.

278. Ben Gurion's dream may be a model village. A little oasis around a few very expensive research institutes. The desert remains a desert. At best, they can stop it from spreading.

Israel cannot take in all of the world's Jews. Nor do all of the world's Jews want to come. European Jews sense that if they came here, it would behoove them to keep quiet about not liking certain things, certain things that were better at home.

Wherever you are, you must share the local community's package of prejudices and self-deceptions. Having traveled this way and that in the world, I had no trouble reaching the conclusion that I would not wish to be at home anywhere else, I wouldn't like to be something other than what I am, a Hungarian Jew.

Thus I am not obligated to take part in any kind of sullen group mendacity, at most in a bit of politeness. Every community is sick of the offenses by its neighbors. The Arabs of Gaza learned that their home does not become paradise if the Jews leave and the Arabs remain, together with themselves, with one another, with their own community.

Nor did Hungary become a paradise when the Soviets left. It is our own ugliness we see in the mirror, if we see ugliness.

279. A new alliance after separation? The declaration that there can be no negotiation in the matter of Jerusalem is not convincing to the rest of the world. When the Israelis grant autonomy, there is justice to the supposition that the Palestinians won't be satisfied, because they want an independent state. In the end, will we see an alliance of states, Israel-Palestine, with its joint capital in Jerusalem?

280. This city, Bersheva, is a model of antiurbanism with good intentions. Enormous space, great waste. Vast amounts of material utilized. Endless housing projects. There's no reason to leave the house, because there's nothing out there. Nothing itself, iden-

tical apartment blocks, separate, with a shopping center placed discreetly here and there, same as at home in Hungary. Etatist functionalism.

A person should drive or take the bus to work and then go home to his family. Modern urban architecture. No articulation, no centers, you are never inside, surrounded by the city. Walking along the streets, you are always outside, outside of the houses, without a compensating feeling even of being "inside" the street.

A long, open room over a good street, with smaller rooms opening from it. In a good city there is interior space outside the house too.

The good city has centrality, a downtown, a thickening cluster. It doesn't have those things if everything is made for cars. Which sight is more important, the human being or the automobile? If the city leadership subordinates everything to cars instead of making downtown a car-free zone, then the citizens have decided in favor of their backsides in a plebeian manner.

Exercising one's legs is permissible; it is worthwhile, because in good cities the street is a series of interesting riddles, it awakens my curiosity, and that makes me want to live.

The city can whet our appetite for life, but it can also dishearten us, depress us. If it bores me, if I do not anticipate anything, if my steps serve to measure only the monotony, if the best I can do is drive from apartment to apartment—I become vapid.

Why are we alive, if it is a matter of indifference where we live or where we are, if our sensual memory has nothing to grasp?

This is what they give immigrants. Let the immigrants be satisfied with it, let them be happy, it's compliments of the state.

281. Every young person wants to be a soldier. Discharged officers can undertake or acquire any federal-public office. The army is the heart of the nation. Multiparty, democratic etatism.

At the first friendly working lunch, I hear stupid jokes about immigrant Russians—the same ones I've been hearing for ten years. My fellow writer, the professor of anthropology, also entertains me with these. Since the Israelis' primary undertaking is the creation of a nation-state, they don't have much left for anything else.

A lucid relationship to institutional clichés, independent of the state—this is the necessary condition for original high culture. This robust collective enthusiasm—it is the hotbed of provincial culture. It is what you get in most countries of the world. Irony is a rare flower, it starts where etatism ends.

The essence of irony is in the alternation of "I'm a part" and "I'm apart." Adult individualism has a flexible lens: I'm with you, I'm on my own. Do you do what is expected of you, or do you do what you expect of yourself?

282. In one Bedouin tent, the wives; in the other, the husband with his guests. Motto: What you would do today, you can do tomorrow too.

What you should do today, postpone until tomorrow. If the wise men make a judgment, they wait three days before proclaiming it, so they can think it over, perhaps it is not just.

It is not bad for them to have lived the same way for thousands of years. Coffee, tea, hashish. To sit on the rug or on the camel's back, and ruminate. If a guest comes, ask him nothing for three days. In my tent he is safe. He cannot be killed here. If he steps outside, that's different.

283. I would like to commemorate the black-hatted van driver who grows tomatoes. The professor who led the excavation and was glad his sick daughter was accepted into the army. The little girl who asked me questions at the airport. The rich American boys, the pompous older brother and the modest younger brother.

The sponsors of the Archaeology Department. They would like to excavate several-thousand-year-old traces of the presence of Israelis, living in luxury. When I am at my best, I'm one with anyone I meet, I have as many selves as I care to produce. I wriggle through and go on my way. The little Pac-man eats everything in his path. If I'm not well, I don't eat people.

1995

Peregrination

284. Was I willing to answer everything honestly? asked the friendly and humorous staff members of the *Jerusalem Literary Project*. They had invited me for a day-long interview, to be filed on CD in the university library in Jerusalem.

Well, of course, as much as possible. I've been honest in every interview, if superficial sometimes. I'm guilty of overdeployment of the ego at times. Yes, I'm ready to answer every question honestly.

The chances of being blown up in Israel are higher, but the danger is more talk than substance; it is statistically insignificant, if we think of the number of traffic accidents. The toll of terror is insignificant.

I risk something by agreeing to the interview, by more or less delivering one of my selves, the Jew, to listeners whom I know hardly or not at all. In all certainty, my Israeli listeners and readers (in contrast to me) identify themselves entirely as Jews and Israelis, while I make them a little nervous. I am the outsider to the insiders, as becomes evident from my frequently being asked why I live where I live. The question comes up outside the context of the interview as well.

285. I live in Hungary not only because I have the right to do so—I reply—though that would be enough. I live there also because I've got used to it, because it turned out this way. I've earned it too; I've done a thing or two for the country. This is the language I speak, and my parents, grandparents, and great-grandparents are buried here.

Most of my ancestors were Jews from the county of Bihar, but a few came from Czech lands too, they settled in Nagyvárad and Berettyóújfalu. And they branched out to points far away. On one side, for example, we have rabbis in Trier, Manchester, and New York. The family has scattered: my daughter lives in Paris, my older sister lives in New York, and I have cousins all over the place. It is a given that not Hungary or America or France or Israel became the integrating home of the family. We live on the earth, at various colorful spots on the globe.

Why are we Jews? Because we were born that way. Because our ancestors were Jews, as far back as we know. This state of affairs was never questionable for me. The idea of converting didn't come up even on Christmas 1944, when nuns of a certain convent would have given us refuge had we been willing to convert. With regard to conversion, I like the conduct of rabbis better; they aren't eager to attract new faithful, they prefer to send away those who apply. "Come back later sometime, if you really want to." Through a series of rejections, it becomes clear whether the applicant is driven by resolute will or just acting on a whim.

286. A Jew has a place anywhere in the world where there are stars over his head. A Jew? A person. Any kind of person. But a Jew is made more adaptable to austere conditions by his portable religion and the relatively broad spectrum granted him in the interpretation of text.

Individual Jews are strengthened by the special interpersonal relationship the prophets established with the voice of God. The prophets' example liberated other Jews to imitate them. As it became a technique of prayer (or actually grew from that), this friendship with God doubled the selves of all Jews. One self is the word of the frail, the other the word of the law, duty, the Unnameable, who entrusts man with an enormous task, to live under the rule of his conscience.

287. The Jew carries the real ruler in himself: the Lord, who is within, instilling him with a sense of duty, that tireless slave driver. That's the source of motivation, diligence, and the thirst to know the essence of things. It comes from there being two of us. Being two gives strength. If we are surrounded, if there are many of the enemy, there are still two of us. And He is more powerful than anything, now and always.

My big brother will come, and then you'll be in trouble! And if the Jew is still the one in trouble for now, those hours of inner freedom serve as consolation in the most miserable situations. He can gaze upon the starry sky even from the door of the barn. The greater degree of inner freedom turned into a greater demand for external freedom, which led to argumentative, malcontented behavior in worldly relationships. Revolutionaries full of simmering resentment come to mind.

There are also gentle anarchists, especially in the arts. There is no art without anarchism, which says there is no law here but that of the author, the creator. Nothing that existed before, nothing that is divine, nothing human.

And if the Lord, the other, voices dissatisfaction, we can say to Him: Brother, I don't interfere in your business, you made a world, dictated its laws, tough enough laws, everyone should mind his own business, you have your work, I have mine.

"All right," God says, "do it." But He stands off to the side and watches as the amateur carpenter tries to knock together his own separate law, one in which both the whole and the part make sense, if possible.

I'm struggling, why deny it? He's struggling too, why deny it? Creation works here, falls apart there, in the disorderly workshop of craftsmen applying themselves.

288. I hope the voice of the insolent Jew is audible in the foregoing. In my novels, consciousness moves alongside, above. The narrative protagonist advances together with the active protagonist, though the narrator always knows a little more; they advance as if sewn together into one skin with their angels. Every day, with greater or lesser intensity, they wrestle, like Jacob, like Israel. Some protagonists are avoided by the angel; he sees them and gives a resigned wave from a distance: they won't be around forever.

289. A man continues in his children, his grandchildren, and in everything he leaves them. So they won't have to start from the beginning. But the best we can get from our parents is warm approval, allocated differently by mother and father, and being flung from the nest, which fosters the skill of flying—or let's call it the ability to stand on our own two feet.

For Jews it is natural for the family to come before all else. The God-fearing, sensible Jew can have many children; they are the source of his wife's joy, and his, but he also goes to the places where men congregate—church, café, academy—to talk things over, or maybe just down to the plaza, beside the stone tables. The family is not just a contingency. The family is substance. The thing given that can be turned into the thing chosen. You must serve your child, your progeny. And if you have none, serve the child of a relative, so that our children are not lost. The murdered must be replaced; the souls of the murdered adopt a newborn. We are bonded to our dead relatives as well as to the living ones. We give the dead a place in the house, in the armchair, in the traveling case.

290. The father of the family is allowed to spend time alone, but he cannot count on complete solitude, because there aren't enough real fathers.

There is much perplexity. There is no one to whom one can turn. There are those who malign the genuine article, so there is a great deal of confusion between real fathers and imposters. Of course the difference comes out, in time, when the portion that belongs to fashion becomes obsolete and we look for the portion that's permanent, and it's either there or it isn't. Unbiased testimony is needed. I am a legitimate witness if no relationship clouds my memory or my judgment.

291. As a writer, I am not a Jew. At least according to my intention. As a writer, I am nothing, just my hand moving the pen or two fingers pecking at the keyboard. There is a chalkboard behind my forehead, and if I close my eyes, I see letters written there. That's how sentences start. I string them together inside.

A critic could discover in my texts attributes he classifies as characteristically Jewish. But that would be the work of the critic. If he wanted to, he could prove anything. But he should take into account that the texts were written in Hungarian and are about things that happened to Hungarians, even if they were Hungarian Jews.

A German professor with slightly crazed eyes put a slip of paper in my hands: the plurality of identities is—schizophrenia. Which testifies to a certain naïveté, because I possess this plurality and yet I am not certifiably schizophrenic. In other words, you can drive the cart with more than one horse. Because identity is the horse and consciousness is the driver.

292. And who is the Lord? Someone always ends up above us. For example, a baby that we lift up high, or a bigger child that we put on our shoulders.

I tried to divest myself of everything forced, of all assimilation, of all toadying to beings that stand above me. So that I could get a little peace. So that not too many people could order me around. So that I wouldn't go dumb from my obligations. So that anxiety wouldn't turn me into a spiritual mute.

You see, my wife bosses me around. Aside from her, I do not give anyone power over me. I am intrepidly autonomous in public and a humble, henpecked husband at home. That is my strategy. That is my trick. That is the way I can get a breath of air, the way I am able to have fun, the way I can secure necessary time alone—it is the way I like most.

293. Jerusalem, 10/17/95. The henpecked husband calls his wife again. It makes sense for a line to be open between them, for them to be able to speak to each other anytime, and to laugh over foolishness, the little tidbits of life.

I am sitting in the Mishkenot Shaananim guest house, in my workroom. There's a kitchenette too, a bedroom and bathroom on the upper deck. I drank coffee and orange juice on the covered terrace, among tropical plants, with the person who will interview me tomorrow, and with whom I will be only as honest as I am with the public or the authorities here and at home, only as honest as I will be tomorrow with the Voice of Israel radio and with the newspaper *Haaretz* after that. My hosts do eight-hour interviews with popular Jewish writers; the company is financed by the Rothschild banking house, and Shimon Peres is the honorary president.

They gave me this superb hotel accommodation, opportunities to take walks, and the advice not to go into the old city, which made me sad, because somehow the modern Jewish part of

Jerusalem interests me less than the Arab quarter or the orthodox Jewish quarter, because the Jewish downtown follows the modern Euro-American pattern, and that's fair. The Arabs' new houses look that way too; only the old is different.

294. There is more light now; there are more healthy young people with quite nice faces and figures promenading along Ben Yehuda, the pedestrian mall. In 1986 too there were many people here, even late at night. This was the Mediterranean strip, hair down to the waist, couples clinging to each other, some of the boys wear yarmulkes but that doesn't make their embrace any less thorough. Our hosts are left-wing, they are angry at the religious Israelis, they want to be worldly, the women want equality. They have had enough of fantasies divorced from reality. Both Jews and Arabs are starting to discover reality, namely, that the others are here and they can be neither thrown into the ocean nor resettled to the other side of the Jordan River. Inevitably there remains a radical minority, which, if it is Arab, cannot give up the idea of the liquidation of the state of Israel, and if it is Jewish, cannot resign itself to the handing over of Judea and Samaria and to the division of Jerusalem.

295. My hosts encourage my interviewer to be tactfully provocative, and the main figure of the local television station asks me, through someone else, if he might be polemical, now, on Friday night, when I read a text aloud. What might he mean by polemical? Probably the question is: Why do I live in Budapest and not here? To which I answer: What I have done up to my sixty-third year, I will not change, unless I really must. I would rather defend my rights in the place where I live.

I am able to defend myself individually, that is a function of my craft and what others think of me. I am glad if I am recognized in Israel as a Jewish writer, because I am that; I am glad if I am recognized in Hungary as a Hungarian writer, because I am that. If someone argues my Jewishness or Hungarianness, I say, Have it your way. One whose passion is calling into question the identity or identities of another person is not of sound mind.

296. Of course, no one is exactly as he says he is. No one is completely this or that—thank God. Everyone is something else as well. The denial or removal of this *something else* commits violence against ourselves and others. The *something else* is the extra, it takes us toward unknown frontiers, it is what makes us specimens of the human race.

If we put the mania of Jewish identity into parentheses just like other identities, is there an experimental result or analyzable result, a test outcome common to the works of Jewish authors, one that gives meaning to their classification as a spiritual-intellectual community?

The answer is precisely the subject under discussion: problematic, paradoxical, dialectical, plural, individually constructed, multifaceted identity.

Jews surge past the given in the direction of some kind of transcendence. They are attracted to universal perspectives, to that which is beyond the border; to disputation or condemnation of the status quo. Their critical relation to the status quo of the human community is an attribute that appears in the texts of the prophets.

They feel divine truth behind them; they each want to find their own connection between daily affairs and the Almighty or the spirit of world history, through the continuous juxtaposition of the abstract and the triflingly particular.

They are curious. Jews have always spread out, going where others have not gone, both in space and in spirit; they are characterized by the urge to experiment, to try some original method or business idea; by the notion that borders can be crossed, bypassed;

by the conviction that it is possible to escape from a seemingly in-escapable place; by the belief that one can extricate oneself from the dead-end street, that it is possible to leave the ghetto.

297. As soon as the exterior environment became less hostile, the ghetto became a network. But the ghetto was and has re-mained to some extent a place of self-isolation, even in the era of networking. Suspicion of the others is still there, misgivings that they, too, might be among the Jew haters. Perhaps those others think Jews should not exist, or at least not this way, not the way they are. They would restrict them with friendly criticism: "Don't bustle, don't occupy the first rows."

Jews must pay for their achievements.

In regions where there is envy, anti-Semitism survives, and the Jews incite it precisely through their assimilation or their inte-gration, by mastering the competitive fields that the surrounding society establishes and achieving good positions in them.

Jews do not grow up to be street sweepers, because the intel-lectual capital accumulated through many thousands of years is passed on to the descendants. The sensitivity, constitution, and probably the nature of our intelligence are all summed up in the gene cocktails that are our children. It is a portable legacy, and it can be operated anywhere.

The majority of Jews cannot help but live in the Diaspora. Wherever they are, they concentrate in the intellectual, scientific, financial, legal, literary, and media fields, in other words, they irri-tate, arouse suspicion and anti-Semitism, because their sheer exis-tence creates tension within the majority's portrait of itself.

298. Danilo Kiš says that being a Jew is an alienation in itself. However, we could also think that being a Jew is not just punish-ment, tribulation, misfortune. Inside a Jew resides an internation-alist, an Israeli nationalist, and another type of nationalist or

regionalist, if the individual does not live in Israel—a Hungarian nationalist, for example.

Perhaps this relative ease in changing points of view makes it more difficult for Jews blindly to forget themselves in raging or quiescent xenophobia. There are murderous Jews, but Jews were more often the killed than the killers.

Naturally, every identity is a limitation at the same time; Jewish identity is too, just because it is Jewish. That is, it is missing something that it is not. Belonging to any people is a kind of naïveté. We could say the same about every kind of belonging; our geographical, civic, and familial attributes all mark our boundaries and our poverty at the same time, the vast territories of our ignorance. Purely by being A, I must suffer the loss of B.

299. Jews did not have the opportunity to become ingrained in a house or a garden over many generations. Rootedness in the earth or, if you prefer, the consoling inner world and the mythology of being tied to the land cannot be characteristic of diaspora peoples, of those who are often exiled.

300. Without the preservation of tradition, no people can exist. I have in mind not only scientific, reflexive preservation, not only the historian's work, but also the ordinary person's way of life. To be a religious Jew means freely deciding to follow the norms our ancestors codified at one time, a few hundred or even a few thousand years ago, and we privilege this immutable permanence of habit over the propositions of changing times. Thus following the religious law becomes more important than our personality; our individuality is then only one of the methods of living consecrated to the Everlasting according to the law.

301. The second path is nation-state sovereignty supported militarily as well as religiously, a position that helps prevent a

second mass slaughter or at least contrasts the ethics of the Masada fortress defenders or the Warsaw ghetto uprising with the role of the submitting victim, a role to which Jews were led by inner fear in addition to outer menace. They did not approve of resistance, because their loyalty to the country that first integrated them and now suddenly rejected them was stronger. After all, the price of their emancipation was respect for the law. The second path, therefore, is collective self-defense and the dignity of standing together: Jewish national consciousness.

302. The third path, the one most typical of Diaspora Jews, is worldly humanism, which can be loyal to the place or nation it attempts to join, but it is freed from local prejudices, partly through being excluded, and chooses not another local prejudice but, rather, something broader, a framework that makes it acceptable to stay for generations, and to enrich the culture of the environment, while making an effort to see beyond the national boundaries.

303. Naturally, three non-Jewish responses are also possible. The first is conversion, perhaps even creation of the concept of Catholic universalism—in other words, the work of Paul and its faithful continuation or at least ostensible acceptance. The second, in the modern era, is nationalist identification with the host nation. The third is internationalism, such as Marxist socialism or even the transnational realism of worldly disciplines.

304. Jewry must understand the multipolarity carried in its very being, the three-pronged road of "authentic and inauthentic" choices. The choice is not authentic if we reject Jewishness, deny it, conceive of it as a weight, a cross, a barrier—in a word, if we try to assimilate to the environment fully. The Jew can convert to another religion; this is the radical counterpole of orthodoxy. The Jew can choose another national consciousness, and he can choose an internationalism that requires the denial of his na-

ture as a Jew; such was communism. The first of the authentic choices is the feudal: segregation from the non-Jewish or the non-Orthodox, from the adulterating medium. It is accompanied by ignoring the outside world, by being closed in and suspicious. Jewish nationalism and worldly universalism can also be accompanied by blindness and lack of communication with other viewpoints. In their lives, Jews look for a compromise between the three choices, and it is interesting to see the individual reactions to this, the trinity built into Jewish existence, the choices of which to place first: prayer, nation, or world. All three answers are whole worlds, and we do not have the right to rank them according to a priority of values.

305. I am also the son of the Hungarian people, my life has been passed in the world of the Hungarians, my ancestors are Hungarian Jews. My country of birth, my native language, my religion, and my family origins are things that I cannot and do not even want to change. The most convenient choice is to accept myself as I am, with this moderate complexity.

306. For those not interested in experiencing themselves as multifaceted beings, Jewishness is a schizoid condition, a severing of the "warm home experience." But who in this world has been given that?

In any case, it is interesting to meet Jews from other countries and find common ground right away. *Sei gesund,* says the Belorussian-Jewish taxi driver in Los Angeles, and it warms my heart, because in this man's smile and in his philosophizing I feel the familiarity of kinship.

307. In the eyes of the person poured from a single mold, plural identity or plural belonging—the person with multiple strategies—is demonic. The ethos of singular belonging and the ethos of plural belonging each creates negative myths about the other.

To the singular, the plural is unfathomable; to the plural, the singular is earthbound.

A Jew can escape from his ambivalence—or polyvalence—only with difficulty. Such escape favors the development of all sorts of egomania. In consequence, we are vexing and well advised to prepare for others' being vexed.

308. The existence of Jews is provocative. The Jewish concept of God is provocative. The challenge cannot be terminated from within or from without; it has to be lived with, along with the reaction to the provocation. Neither assimilation nor Auschwitz are appropriate solutions to the problem. The problem of this provocation must be faced.

Why don't they dissolve into the surrounding majority? Why don't they give themselves over completely? Why do they identify with the passions of their environment only partially and conditionally?

Why isn't the Jew Christian? Why isn't the Jew Muslim?

309. If the national, ethnic, and religious spheres are unified into one among other peoples, that is unpropitious for the Jews, because it increases their exclusion. The Jews themselves, however, have connected national, ethnic, and religious consciousnesses in the state of Israel.

310. No one has sure answers to the most unsettling questions. Rabbis do not have a monopoly on Jewish consciousness, nor do Israeli politicians. The *whole* of Jewish literature can be conceived of as nothing more than an experimental approach, taking into account that one characteristic of literature is authors' being necessarily limited by their singularity, even if they have traveled somewhat farther than others on the road to understanding.

311. In the afternoon, on the way back from a long ramble, I went through the showy, Western, Jewish downtown, then through Mea Shearim and through the Armenian and Christian quarters in the old city. I sat at a Jewish café on a square, I did the same at an Armenian café called Jerevan in the old city, then at a Muslim Arab café at the Damascus Gate. Last night, they warned me not to enter the old city, especially not alone. Naturally I entered, but I was a little scared. I had a good conversation with two friendly Arabs.

The western city, the worldly Jewish Jerusalem, is like a number of cities in the Mediterranean basin: speeding cars, a few skyscrapers, shiny bank portals, many car rental agencies, some places with more garbage than others, more disorder, quarters made chaotic by construction, then palm trees again, fountains, donations that have become parks and wonderful scenes in side streets, many little eateries not doing too much business, a flood of tourists, who make local behavior international and steer it toward the catering industries.

312. The Orthodox quarter is just the opposite. There, they didn't see me at all, it is a perfectly closed society, they do not see what does not belong to them. I looked at them; they didn't look back, they were deep in incomprehensible exertions, they made shoddy refrigerators operational, sold devotional items, ugly shoes, and sweets. I saw many ugly people with bad physiques and many beautiful people whose faces reflected deep thought. I saw delicate, used-up, sad women; lots of children; men with troops of their kids; groups of children standing on the side of the street, playing soccer, crying in stairways, chattering on terraces and in little yards. The little boys wore yarmulkes and long sidelocks curled into tubes. Strangest were the men in wide fur caps and knee pants; one might say that their uniforms were as interesting as those of the Royal Guards. Compared to them, the

women are mousy. The Orthodox men are festive cocks, their wives inconspicuous hens.

Both the bourgeois and the religious quarter were very familiar to me. Familiar faces from my distant past. I saw them in the more affluent, greener quarter as well as in Mea Shearim buildings pasted together anarchically of stone, tin, and boards; in the software store for Torah scholars, with compact discs containing the Talmud.

Abstraction is everything to these people. Their worldly, corporeal lives: the maintenance of what was. They have banks, they must get their merchandise from somewhere, but everything is as it was before the war. The faces in the recesses of the shops are like those that were in Berettyóúfalu.

The enormous market with its rows of stalls. Everything is juxtaposed there, silk scarves and fish, olives and chicken legs, great slabs of beef and Hebrew signs, a great quantity of seeds, nuts, superb fruits. I drank a lot of fresh-squeezed orange juice and outstanding Turkish coffee with cardamom. It's easy to get by without meat here. The air was alive everywhere. I stepped in dust and sand, walking for almost five hours. I became fresher and fresher. I found a street, walked down it a stretch, then turned, sometimes toward greater traffic, sometimes away from it. My branchings off were intuitive, and as I went, the ugly disappeared, it was also beautiful, it just depended on your point of view.

313. The Orthodox quarter made me respectful: how well they have been able to preserve the past, proudly staying out of modernity, without the slightest inclination to progress. Tradition is enough for them, even if they do use computers to study the ancient texts. The computer is only a tool; the essence is preparation to go before the Lord. This world is incidental to them. They walk deeply immersed in their own thoughts, often with incomprehensible haste. They carry plastic shopping bags with prayer shawls inside.

Maybe they are not all poor, but my impression is that most of them are, that the young father really must think about what he can afford from the toy store, because he has many children. What should he buy for the one who has a birthday, so that the others get something too? He walks around, looks over the merchandise, finds his way into recesses filled with yet more toys, then comes out in front of the store and stands there thinking things over for a long time. He can't have much money in his pocket.

Prayer is more important here than business, but so is conversation. I saw leisurely discussions in cafés and in stores. Suddenly one of the participants would remember something, come out and rush off, in all likelihood for the next world, even if he has to make a stop first in the kitchen, shop, or school.

On some of the faces I see genuine profundity, very fine skin, it brings to mind one of my classmates at the elementary school in Berettyóúfalu, suffocated by gas. He was another one who didn't see anything outside of his imaginings. He was a very serious boy, all his lessons perfect, his handwriting impeccable. I can imagine him here. His beard would be gray by now, he would wear a broad-brimmed black hat, and there would be a long, slightly shiny black coat on his lean figure. The children would surround him, he would discuss something with them quietly, respectfully, then he would continue on his way, with eyes cast down, but not as if he were looking at the asphalt, he would be looking somewhere inside, perhaps at a dark wall; a voice comes from beyond it, reminding him of his errors.

I experience not even a trace of hospitality among these people. Someone like me is an intruder in their part of town, peeping into their lives, something that must be suffered, but in order to make my presence less disturbing, they look right past me. I see a little curiosity in the eyes of the older men. I am no more inclined to join their ranks than those of the Trappist monks, who produce wonderful wine and do not speak to one another. I see both monkish lifestyles as beautiful, the familial and the solitary.

314. I saw many different kinds of communities, some more sympathetic than others. It never crossed my mind to curry favor and try to join them, but I looked at all of them with interest, perceiving myself everywhere as guest rather than local. I have to confess I felt most at home in the Arab café at the Damascus Gate. The boss and his wife—clipping their daughter's nails—were both kind and encouraged me to come again. I also liked seeing how two young men, evidently close acquaintances, came in, respectfully shook hands with the boss's wife, and kissed the child with real kindness.

315. An elderly Arab said that Rabin, Peres, King Hussein, and Mubarak are among the best, because they understood that they must speak to one another and that force will not work, they must live together and work together. The Jews have nowhere to go; to chase them into the ocean would not be nice, and it would not even be possible. They must be regarded as cousins.

316. Yesterday I talked all day long, about my life and about literature, about God, about unpleasant circumstances and happy ones. The air-conditioning worked. I asked for more and more glasses of wine. Sometimes I broke into a sweat, so they powdered me. I will be preserved on a CD, on platinum, in the archives of the Jerusalem University library, I am put away in a bomb-proof place, I have outlived myself.

317. I walked long on the shiny yellow stones in the neighborhood of more sparsely inhabited artist homes purchased by American Jews; I walked slowly, dragging myself along. I'll never have the money for such a house. The concrete half globes of David Village stand opposite the old city. Suleiman's work is more appealing.

I walked among the cars then down into the valley of Gehenna, where there are kitsch painters' studios. At the Jaffa Gate

I sat down in an Arab restaurant called Moses. I ate a contemporary meal: ground meat, mixed salad, fried potatoes, hummus. I drank red wine with it, and Turkish coffee. Then I walked across the Armenian quarter to the Wailing Wall, where the goyim, the men without hats, stared from beyond the cordon, and I stood among them. I could have made a little fuss and been let in, but the handwashing would have stumped me, and I wouldn't have known whether or not to stop at the top of the ramp, bobbing forward rhythmically with my upper body, as many do.

From the terrace of the Moses Restaurant, I watched the parade of religions, this multitude of uniforms. So many kinds of Orthodox wear, so many kinds of Christian orthodoxy, and the multitude of Catholic monks! The tourists flood in, they have a peek at the praying. And the bearded men come in big cars; the men in hats come bumptiously. A costume ball; we tourists go to catch a glimpse, a glimmer of devoutness. It's the costume ball of those bustling around God. But God forbid some syncretism should bring them together, or that they should find common ground! On the contrary, let them differ! Let the nimble Jews run, let the slow Muslims go in their skirts, let the Europeans be curious, let the Americans be officious.

318. I saw tall, stick-thin boys dressed in black, with translucently white faces. If they shake their heads, the sidelocks fly around, twisted into braids, into tubes. There is serious preparation and a pious aesthetic in this. The kind of stocking worn is also important.

They try to make individuality disappear, but if they throw it out the door, it comes in through the window. Only on superficial observation could one think that there is no personality in the Orthodox community, that it consists only of black hats and the recitation, murmuring of the eternal text, swearing loyalty to the Lord, because You are great and I am no one, please, protect me from my enemies!

I have no enthusiasm for this abundance of flattery and pleading, but I do look long at the Wailing Wall and at the bushes growing out of it, and I think of my whole family, wishing them well, as long as I'm standing here at the wall of wishes and wailings.

This is just the place I would not be inclined to cry, since emotion is on display here: to bow in a big fur cap, to stand in the corner, where the density of white beards, black hats, and long coats is the greatest, to bend down and straighten up in one rhythm before the Lord. Those who do so think the sight pleases God. Elderly men run to get here before the Sabbath begins.

For my part, I have never joined any kind of square dance or group sing, or only if I was coerced. Where the spirit of community thrives, I make myself scarce.

319. I'm starting to walk badly, limping and feeling increasing pain in my left knee, but I continue, it is my passion. After an hour or two, the body becomes lighter, the legs more limber, and one always sees something strange, though one must make allowances for safety. One is afraid on a street with no sidewalk, where crazed cars rumble past.

320. I drag myself home, go to bed, wake up, drink coffee, squint. I am weak. I cough. I lean back and forth. In the newspaper I read that the government has given the security forces another three months of permission to interrogate, and that the terrorists are increasingly expert as well. Some say there will be peace, others say no. The crazy Jews and the crazy Arabs run beside each other, this one bows, that one bows, and the Catholics kneel. And I lock my hands together behind me, though I would like to kick the habit. I plan to have a long night. I would like not to be woken by coughing, the impulse to urinate, sweating, the many imperfections of the body. Before I lie down to sleep for the night, I go out to the long, colonnaded porch corridor, where

red photocells indicate that someone has stepped out, and the monitor shows him walking up and down.

I am still tired from the long interview. I talked for eight hours. I have grown sick of words in my mouth, I don't even want to hear human speech. I use my eyes now more. I have succeeded in speaking to no one all day; the silence following so much talk begins to bring me back into balance. Tomorrow night, however, I have to give my reading.

1995

Three Roads for Jews

321. Jewish modernization, embourgoisement, and secularization progressed in parallel to those of Christians. The processes were doubled in force, because Jews had to come out from behind a Christian as well as a Jewish wall. From an orthodox point of view, or as seen by the unfriendly eye of the environment, this was quite a rapid assimilation. In Central Europe, Christian embourgoisement was also quite a rapid assimilation: the absorption of foreign models, technologies, skills, fashions. The citizen becomes connected to the world at large, and gets his goods wherever he can find them. Christian and Jewish citizens together created the Central European bourgeois lifestyle, using the international model, with heavy local coloring.

In becoming bourgeois, the Jews lost Hebrew, Yiddish, Ladino, then because of the Germans' ugly behavior they lost literary German too as a common language and identified culturally with the people in whose region or state they lived. Hungarian Jews spoke Hungarian, Romanian Jews spoke Romanian, Polish Jews spoke Polish, and Czech Jews spoke Czech, even in their dreams. The notion of isolating themselves culturally did not even come up.

322. The cohabitation of ethnic minorities and majorities is always symbiotic. From the standpoint of modernization, the Jewish presence had a productive effect on local societies. The same energy was at work in Jews as in the surrounding people: to be liberated from their own feudalism, from the ghetto that was made impermeable for those within as well as for those without. To be free of segregation, to break out of the cell closed by external regulations and inner definitions! The individual's emancipation from the religious community, from the church, was part of European embourgeoisement. Whether the religious organization was hierarchical or communal, it fit the person of the feudal era rather tightly. Jewish emancipation was driven by an eruption of emotion: from now on, let it be possible for us to have contact with every other person on the globe, let us really be neighbors to our neighbors.

323. Neither assimilation nor dissimilation would be a precise word for the process presently taking place among Central European Jewry. The more thoughtful take seriously both (or more) of their identities and do not want to deny either identity for the sake of the other. They do not wish to decide the question of whether they are Jewish Hungarians or Hungarian Jews. They can view themselves either way or neither way. The majority of Jews I know believe that a Jew is a person who thinks and says he is a Jew. Non-Jews rarely assert that they are Jews.

324. I haven't yet met "Jewry" or the "Hungarian nation," only people, some like this, some like that. If they are killed, Jews are all the same. Otherwise, if they are permitted to live, they are all different. In the cattle trains and barracks, they also started to become the same. As civilians, before and afterward, they were different. The sensibility of reduction to a common essence is a product of the machinery of the *Endlösung*.

325. For centuries, Jews have been guests vested with the rights of guests wherever they reside, because they think of themselves as guests instead of choosing complete assimilation. Unsuccessful patterns of assimilation cannot be duplicated; neither the Christian-national nor the Communist-socialist strategy of assimilation proved workable. Jews cannot free themselves from the gift, or from the burden, of having been born Jews.

Jews live like those in their environment, but they are interested in the fact that they are Jews. In any case, they will be made to understand, in many ways, that they differ, that they are the other. Not a week passes without a newspaper item or graffiti to remind them of it. They read a brief report on the destruction and defacing of some tombstones, and it will not leave their minds along with the other brief reports. One night, they are full of hope that they will find a peaceful home in the place, where they are; the next night, they are seized by doubt; the third night, they reflect that it has been this way for thousands of years and probably will stay this way for quite a while still.

326. It doesn't hurt to repeat: the Jewish question is the Christian or Muslim society's question. How well do they tolerate themselves? If they tolerate their own diversity, then they will tolerate the Jews too. If they want to oppress themselves, then they will rage against the Jews as well. According to the signs, Central European societies do not wish to oppress themselves on the eve of the third millennium; in other words, they can coexist with Jews.

If democracy becomes stable in Central Europe, then the non-Jews will live with Jews without any trouble. I presume that the authoritative middle-class in Hungary, for example, will prefer to employ a legal-cultural rather than a religious-racial concept of nation, and will regard as part of the Hungarian people the Jews who live here, are native Hungarian speakers, and are citizens of

Hungary. There will be no public astonishment at the idea that Judaism is transnational like all world religions, like the larger and smaller Christian churches.

In Hungary, for example, there is a viable Jewish community, with schools where children can be Jews naturally; for them, lighting candles at Hanukkah is normal. There are still Jews willing to sustain a world of memory, to nurture the tradition, to operate the temple, and there is a demand for the synagogue to be a kind of classroom after services. In Hungary there are Jewish associations, schools, periodicals, book publishers, readings on Jewish subjects in the shopwindows, and television programs explaining the significance of Jewish holidays. Judaism as a religion or as a historic and established church receives a certain amount of legal recognition. A significant portion of Jews is not religious, another significant portion is religious in its own way; only the most modest portion attends synagogue, and even fewer Jews follow the religious instructions in their daily life.

327. Hungarian Jews living in Israel return to Hungary to visit, and it is more and more usual for Hungarian Christians to go to Israel. They no longer face a phantom; they face, rather, a people who love and fear for their homeland, just as the visitors do. Hungary has expanding contacts with Israel; I assume they will continue to widen, if only because in Israel as well as Hungary there are numerous Jews who can speak Hungarian. There is a chance that the collaboration of the two nations will supply a new framework for interpreting Hungarian—mainly Budapest—Jewry, whose conduct and fate is paradigmatic if only because it is the largest Jewish community in Central Europe. The broadening of Israeli-Hungarian contacts is a sensible prediction, and every kind of exchange is an important part of it: bilateral tourism, with visits to Hungarian cemeteries, culinary delights, and the passion of Hungarian-speaking Israelis for theater. It is also natural for

Israelis, who are mainly Eastern European in origin, to become interested in their place of origin. It is increasingly natural for Christian Hungarians to visit the land of the Bible and, if they happen to be fruit farmers, to see how their Israeli counterparts go about their work. It is impossible for the more receptive not to be moved by the biblical land. Modern Israel is also worth seeing. So, this is the kind of country these Jews have made! Considering what they began with, it is more than worthy of attention. But more important: it is a humanly comprehensible country. That is, Jews become comprehensible as people through it. And in the context of such everyday contact, anti-Semitic mythologies have nothing more meaningful to say about Jews than Dracula films have to say about Transylvania.

328. If Central Europe stays pretty much the way it is, or if it gets a little better—in other words, if there will be imperfect and stumbling but reliable democratic states of law there—then several alternatives are open to the Jews who wait and remain. The Jews, as a national or ethnic minority, did not organize themselves into political associations or parties, they do not stand up for collective rights, they forgo the kind of reverse discrimination that is demanded by other national minorities. They do not wish to isolate themselves or segregate themselves, they do not ask for autonomy—beyond the civil rights of association that belong to everyone, or beyond the rights that are due all churches. Over and above the demand for democratic rights, Jewry cannot be perceived as a political interest group. It is normal for there to be conservative, liberal, and socialist Jews. They move in many different directions and have no common political denominator other than requiring democratic freedoms. If there is liberal democracy, then there are Jewish organizations and Jews who have nothing to do with the Jewish organizations. To belong or not belong to an organization is not a life-or-death question.

It is clear that Jews' interests are on the side of liberal democracy, of a constitutional state of law where they and other citizens are legal subjects with equal rights. Jews' interests are opposed to all antidemocratic nationalism. Where the majority angrily restricts any minority is a bad place for Jews. The rights of Jews are in good shape in countries where it is not possible to kill people simply out of political considerations, to rob them with official authorization, and bureaucratically to take them out of circulation. Jews' interests are in democracy at every level: local and national, transnational and transcontinental, over the entire globe, everywhere they go, and not only in political terms but also in interpersonal relationships. In the modern era, a life that follows the Ten Commandments is most possible in liberal democracies. If a Jew labors to weaken democracy, one may doubt his soberness of judgment.

329. In the twentieth century, the dispersion of Jews increased in range and effect, but in extermination camps and as victims, Jews also played exceptional, globally significant roles. After Auschwitz, no matter what Jews say about their own Jewishness, they must think about it; neither they nor their descendants can forget it.

The lesson of Jewish vulnerability and helplessness in World War II is that Jews must become strong and show strength. This applies not only to the Israeli Jews coalesced into a nation but also to the Jews of the Diaspora. They must be committed adherents of fundamental human rights everywhere on earth, because that is the guarantee of their survival. In this respect, they are in solidarity with every people, every minority that stands up for its own fundamental human rights using nonviolent means.

330. The supplemental energy generated by carrying a paradox identity fuels most Jewish achievements. Jews have gone far

in individualization. What is nevertheless common to Jews? Only that they declare themselves Jews.

No matter what language they speak, Jews recognize one another with few words, their relationships to one another are more emotional, more fraternal, and more volatile. They meet with non-Jews and have contact with them, but they do not blend in completely. They do not proselytize, and most of them do not convert either. They respect God by remaining Jews. They have undertaken a conspicuous role in the connection of the world through communication, in telecommunications, commerce, intellectual dialogue, in the transformation of the earth and of those living on it.

331. In order to think of Judaism as our own, we must think of it as unfinished, as something that changes with us. We do not identify it entirely with priestly speech. Everyone who calls himself a Jew is entitled to redefine the word.

The Christians received the Jewish tradition through Jesus. Jesus takes Jewishness with him into the entire Christian world. Prophets, apostles, and saints are visible on a church fresco. Even if they want to, Christians and Jews cannot separate their most important words and images.

Through Christianity and Islam, Jews have given a significant portion of humanity an important period in their own ancient history. Living scattered throughout the world can be viewed as a calamity, but also as part of a divine plan. The world as one, and the notion that people are capable of understanding one another, follows from Jewish monotheism. Jews may view having to be able to exist anywhere as a fulfillment of their duty.

332. There are Jews almost everywhere on earth; there is not another people that has scattered as much, been exterminated as much, and yet survived as much; that is their extraordinariness.

Their survival over time and the continuity of their persecution are historical facts. The appearance of Jews as a global people in the realm of symbols is a historical fact. It is the only global people, and that is the root of its mission. A global people in nation-states, this is the Jewish paradox.

333. Jews integrated into national cultures learned the various intimacies of those national cultures. Jews consider themselves a global people, and at the same time they adjust to the national environment they inhabit. On the one hand, universalism, on the other, that strange people with its own religion. There are many historical peoples who would like to have their own religion; they presume it would be a good thing to have. Many Jews, however, are not convinced that it is good for them. They would be satisfied with a somewhat less conspicuous role. But even if they try, they cannot hide their nature; the paths of denial have been flops. The Jews are one of the oldest peoples, and one that continually has to reinvent itself.

334. The people that chose itself for the priestly role preserved its distinctness while advocating the idea of a single God and a single mankind. The task of the priestly people is to establish spiritual-intellectual contact with all the peoples of the earth and to bring the faiths and worldviews into dialogue.

With Babel, God created diversity, so that it wouldn't be easy for us to understand one another, and so that it would take work for us to understand the unusual. Without the unusual, the common is meaningless. At the same time the divine instruction is to bring the world together, to understand one another, to serve the cause of peace between peoples, and to keep awake respect among fellow men.

Have we perhaps reached the end of optimistic universalism, with its agenda including resolution of differences, bridging gaps, association, integration? Will the neoromanticism of communal isolation put an end to the mood that favors spiritual meetings of religions and nations, meetings on some indeterminate plane indicated by the single God of the Jews?

335. Originally, of course, it really was the God of only one people, but it did not stay that way, and the works of modern Jews have made them conveyors of a universalist mode of thinking, one that transcends them. This irresolvable duality is the lot of the Jews, to live between the global and national perception of self, this fretting and ambivalence, the universal challenge and the loneliness of minority.

336. The spiritual is beyond illustration; it is forbidden to depict the one and only God in pictures, but the language of the Bible is all pictures. Hebrew words can be interpreted in several different ways because of the way they are written. This stimulates debate and hints that things can be viewed in more than one way. Consequently there is no institutionally authorized repository of truth. The Jewish religion gives prophets and wise men distinguished roles; there are not many, but there are some, in any case more than one, therefore we can select among their wisdom as we select among the classics according to our age and mood. The outstanding writer (as all prophets are) is granted religious rank. The role of the autonomous interpreter is sanctified, and thus the Jewish faith allows a great degree of individualization: masters have exceptional influence on thinking.

337. The works of worldly Jews have become part of Jewish culture; religious Judaism is just another part. In the reality of the spirit, there is no place for a sharp frontier between religious and worldly meditation. Literature by nature ignores that border. It empowers the frail teacher who distinguishes himself

from his environment with clear-sightedness in the light of grace and divines the Lord's intention. One may legitimately place religious literature into the tradition of literature, and declare that books written by worldly Jews from Spinoza to Kafka and beyond are part of the Jewish tradition, part of Judaism as well.

For worldly Jews, Jewish literature does not stop with the Torah and the Talmud. The past one and a half thousand years have also provided a few pages of Jewish authors that could be placed alongside the sacred texts.

338. One must count on the divine anarchy residing in man. I say divine, because God laughs at our constructions. In Jews one can count on encountering apostates, prophets, rebellious angels, the courage to say of the point where any of us happens to be standing, here and now: This is the beginning, the place of origin, the zero point. When we are at the zero point of knowledge, placed there metaphysically by our finiteness and frailty, it doesn't even occur to us to teach or preach.

The real direction of transcendence is not the beyond, the other world, not beyond the earth, but rather the multiplication of living bodies, the family. That is why the child is at the top of the scale of values. The parent lifts the child above himself/herself, surviving the trials of today and personal death through descendants who don't yet have names. The parent upholds the Ten Commandments, contravenes them, puts them back in place: the parent cannot ignore the Covenant.

339. Jewishness has three distinct poles: the religious community, Israel, and worldly individualism. These poles appear to deny one another; in reality they are interdependent and nurture one another. In any case it requires a generous kind of wisdom for them to be able to coexist in dignity, even within a single

consciousness or biography. One might say that all three poles require a whole person.

The first path: orthodoxy, the preservation of the tradition, not only in books but also in life practices that accept being separate from other people, in familial monkdom, in wanting immutable customs in spite of changing times—in a word, a completeness that cannot easily be integrated with the philosophies of the other two poles.

The second path is national modernization, the sovereign Jewish state capable of defending itself, deterring further anti-Jewish mass murders; collective self-defense, the dignity of standing up for ourselves together as opposed to the resigned martyrdom of the Shoah's helpless victims. Building up the state of Israel can fill a person like the national consciousness that belongs to it.

The third path is the secular individualism of Jews living in the Diaspora. I speak not of giving up Jewish consciousness and identity, not of converting to another religion, not of nationalist or Communist assimilation. I speak of the economic, scientific, and artistic achievements with which Jews living in various countries and language communities have enriched the surrounding cultures and universal culture.

340. Globalization and the interweaving of the world go forward, and Jews always play the avant-garde role in this, irritating the surrounding majority. Localism is always mad at them, because they are translocal. The borders of the state are not the borders of existence for them, they do not think of everything beyond the border as foreign and hostile; after all, the environment within the border is not especially friendly to them either.

The global people turns up everywhere, using its head, initiating, and writing books in conspicuous numbers. We must be aware of the two sides of our spirit: locality and universality, belonging and not belonging. It is precisely this ambivalence that gives Jewish irony its tension.

It is plausible for a Jew to compare peoples and to see one in another. Jews, like yeast, are in constant motion relative to others, and they are at home on the road, like the Mr. Cohen of jokes, who feels good neither in the country he emigrates from nor in the country he emigrates to. Jews are not masters at the tranquillity of staying in place.

Partly as a consequence of discrimination against them, secular humanist Jews are disengaged from the main local prejudice, and they do not choose another local prejudice but, rather, look for something broader, a validity more universal than the national.

341. Jewry cannot help but understand the multipolarity inherent in its existence. Certain Jews can even like their multipolarity, viewing it as romantic and mysterious. We may give up the misconception that one pole is true and proper, able to contain and replace the other two, which appear less true and proper. It is natural for Jews to search for compromise between these three options in their personal or family life, and it is quite interesting to see what a person puts first—prayer, the country, or the world—and what has to be given up in consequence. To those who cannot understand this multipolarity and cannot even enjoy it as an aesthetic experience, being Jewish is a burden, too complicated, almost a schizoid state. The strategy of a people is the sum of the life strategies of its individuals. The Diaspora is a given, as is universalization, and Jewish participation in universalization.

342. Which necessarily has its distorted negative image: the anti-Semitic myth of Jewish conspiracy for world dominion, a theme we can find anywhere in the world. A suspicious, primitive mind-set regards plural identity as demonic and dangerous: it is there and not there; if it is here, it is not just here; perhaps it is

from another planet. A Jew has trouble freeing himself from his polyvalence, his plurality of values. He is incurably more at home in the land of paradox and irony, and therefore provokes the resentment of the local community.

343. The element of provocation cannot end with the establishment of the state of Israel, since the existence of Israel in the Near East, in the Arab-Islamic world, is no less provocative than the existence of the Jewish minority in the Euro-American Christian world.

344. The existence of Jewry, its concept of God, is itself the provocation that nothing stops. Why isn't the Jew Christian, why isn't he Muslim, why is the Jew Jewish anyway? Why does he not dissolve into the surrounding majority and its particular world-view? There is no rational answer to this question. Because he doesn't! Just because! And it will remain so for a few thousand years more.

345. I repeat, it is not easy to view with understanding and sympathy the contradictory and complimentary relationship among Jewry's three authentic strategies. Without Jewish consciousness, we are not capable of self-irony and constructive, judicious compromises.

346. The basis of Jewish consciousness is not Auschwitz but this three-pronged enterprise, this strategic triad: tradition, nation, world. It is all there in the sacred writing: the priestly, the national, and the prophetic-universal.

Jews received from fate the skill of changing perspective and with it the empirical clue to the whole of mankind. They have also been taught that they must defend themselves in all their forms.

One cannot give up universalism, which is the radical consequence of monotheism. Furthering of the tradition and opening toward the future are equally divine commands. We have about as much time to work on the realization of this paradoxical task as humankind has on earth, perhaps a few thousand years more. By accepting the plurality of our being, we can assist humanity in awakening to itself.

Approaching David

347. Glory to the chosen one! Woe to the chosen one! And woe to those who are not chosen! The chosen are chosen. Did the one the Lord wanted become king? Did the Lord want the one who became king?

The old prophet wanted the very last child, the handsome young shepherd who dispatched even bears and lions, to protect his sheep. The prophet anointed the boy. The boy didn't stay a shepherd for long.

Perhaps the Lord chose David because He heard the songs of the lute-playing boy. The anointed one discovers hidden resources within himself. He learns to win. He is the chief accepted by the army, the priesthood, the elders, and the corps of prophets. There are fortunate constellations, when an appropriate candidate and a keen-eyed jury converge.

The magic coat of the chosen one is others' faith in him. But one must know how to wear the coat.

The one who can chase away the evil spirit by dancing and plucking the lute, the one who frequently turns to the Lord and hears the message urging him to act or be still—he is surrounded by the mystique of victory, which does half the work, but the chosen one is responsible for the other half.

In other words, being chosen is not a permanent attribute but, rather, help, circulation of divine grace, requested and received by the hour and by the minute. It can be cut off for good at any moment. The poor chosen one must feel that every minute might be the last one, that the next step might not work, that the Lord might withdraw His approval.

As long as the chosen one enjoys the confidence of the Lord, however, there is a radiant period when the young champion ascends, when he is sheltered by the luminous shield of virtue rather than by heavy copper armor. But the going gets harder, because the hero of the story is surrounded by innumerable temptations to do wrong.

The aureole of victory is like a rainbow in the sky.

The price of glory is woe.

348. If Jesus—who appeared one thousand years after David and was said to be the king (at least spiritually) of Israel—is descended from David, according to Jesus's biographers, then his is not just royal lineage but also lineage from the ideal King, then the Christian church can be regarded more or less as one of the branches of the church founded by David, since Jesus too would have liked to preach his truth in the Jerusalem temple built by David and Solomon in Jerusalem.

On the Temple mount, at its base or in its immediate vicinity, are rocks, caves, and buildings sacred to three religions. Jesus appeared before the monument wrought by David and Solomon, the father-king and the son-king, and Muhammad flew up from there too. Jesus and Muhammad both went up to the sky. The bodies of David and Solomon remained in the earth where they were buried. There is no report of their ascending to heaven. They were both worldly kings, and they lived through the most important events of worldly tales.

349. David? He is the first king that is truly a king, the first one

to pass through all the stations of a man's life. David is the ancient man-image, the shepherd become poet-king, the fairy-tale third son, actually not even the third but the seventh, in a word, the child of the Sabbath, Jesse's holiday child.

He starts off innocent; he has fought, but he has not yet killed a man, just lions and bears, almost with his bare hands. He fought them to defend his sheep.

He is tempted and falls into sin, he is contrite and punished in love and is a polygamist, merciful and cruel, writer of a part of the Psalms, while another part was written in his court.

He unified the country, Israel and Judah, he founded the capital city, created a strong kingdom, and sired Solomon. From David's love came the most able king, who built up the realm he inherited to one of grand scale.

The son of a poet is a poet; the son of David of the Psalms is Solomon, who was called wise, who—according to the narrative permeated by desires—is the author of the Proverbs, which can be used as a handbook of morality, author of the Song of Songs, which the reader can view either as a mystical or sensual love poem, and author of the Book of Ecclesiastes, which advises us that everything has its time and that everything is but vanity.

David is the raw story and the great dream. He is the one who became a statue. He is the one who rose from beside the sheep to the chair of the anointed, the one who became the Christ of the Lord, or Messiah, or king anointed by sacred oil, the guardian of the Ark of the Covenant, the one favored by the priests. He is the one who went from savage tribal fighter to lawgiver and singer of humility before the Lord.

His biographers gave him everything, all the antipodes of life; he was put into every ambiguous and dramatic situation. His story might be the anecdotal heart of the Old Testament. More is written about him than about all the patriarchs together.

David is the realization, with him starts the golden age, he is the moment of celebration, of success. This was the Jews' golden age, turning silver with Solomon, who was mature and saw beyond himself. In this monumental narrative, the patriarchs and Moses the lawgiver are followed by the unification of the realms, and one more glimmer. Then come the storms, the attempts to make islands in space and time, within the Diaspora; illumination and darkening.

350. Regardless of the state of the relationship between Jewry and Christianity, David is the favorite Old Testament hero of Bible readers, the man of practical deeds, not the teacher but the chief who came from down low and reached up high, who knows both the arrogance of power and humility, innocence and the tempting power of sin, but can resist temptation in the name of a higher law.

David lived a complete man's life, he was granted everything a person can have. He danced at the head of the triumphal march, he was like the happy champions at the Olympics, and he could identify himself with God, because the prophet anointed him, and thus his victory was the realization of God's will.

This Jewish dance with the Lord: to separate Him from us as far as possible, to push Him away into abstract infinity, so that He cannot be pulled down to earth, so that no man will even think of mistaking himself for God. It was daring to decide that God is not as we are, and not even like anything we have seen. That idea liberates the human. Then again, there are the prophets with their strict talk. Their contemporaries have a hard time deciding which one is genuine and which one is false, as they all speak in His name.

351. A priestly nation, said God to Moses, thus every Jew feels himself entitled to play the role of intermediary, to engage in dialogue with the Lord, to negotiate continuously between his own

very worldly person and the Almighty, who is supposedly infinite. That is what religion is about, reconciling the humanly finite with the divinely infinite.

If the Lord weren't infinite, He wouldn't demand so infinitely much, then we wouldn't have to regard ourselves and all of mankind as frail creatures made in God's image, creatures who carry the highest thing within themselves.

352. See how many kinds of perfection are discovered in the simple shepherd boy, as if the inspired individual were a mine to be excavated at God's signal. This time God gives a sign to the prophet Samuel: he should not be satisfied with the six brothers that have been brought before him, he should call for the seventh, the realization.

And the last one becomes first—that is the great folk tale. He even becomes king more or less without sin. He could have become king by a thrust of his lance, but he did not do it, because God punishes bloodshed. But spilling blood is the fate of founders, thus they cannot enter the promised land, they do not have the right to build the temple, because they are responsible for too much bloodshed, though they are permitted to place the temple on Mount Zion.

David is an emotional person, he is capable of love and contrition. His bright gaze, the beauty of his face and build were immediately apparent to the old prophet. Samuel understood why the Lord had chosen David, the modest shepherd who tended his flock. David's dignity gradually rises to the kingly level.

353. Saul likes David, who dances before him, but the king throws a lance at the boy. The reflexes of the Lord's favorite are good, however; he knows the art of dodging. David dances and sings before Saul, who is a head higher than the others and also exceptionally handsome. The smaller but more graceful David is

King Saul's esteemed lieutenant, a man of the court, but the feelings that an older chief can feel toward an aspiring one Saul feels now; he cannot bear to admit that he is weaker. The feeling of primacy dwells within the ruler, he cannot bear to step back and become second. Both were praised—to subdue a thousand Philistines is no easy task, but, well, David slew ten thousand, and that was unbearable.

David gives the foreskins of two hundred Philistines to the princess. The circumcision was in all likelihood coupled with murder. David is from the same world as his peers. He does not say his country is not of this world. His country is here, only he, as king, is somewhat better.

David is saddened that Saul—whom he loves, to whom he was loyal, the king to whom God alternately sends good and evil spirits—wants to have him killed. The persecuted one hides in a cave, he sleeps on rocks.

David is saddened to hear that priests have been massacred, together with their families and their livestock, for giving him lodging, food, and a sword; it is a great sadness to bring death to those who were our helpers.

The persecuted one hides away, and a sword is thrust toward him in his cave. When his quickened heart calms down, he feels that everyone is against him, that no one is with him. He doesn't yet know that the kingdom will be his, he is still surrounded by death.

354. The favorite warrior-chief became a rebel marked for death, because he was granted more glory than King Saul. He could kill the king, but he does not raise a hand against God's anointed one. He humbly calls himself a flea, a dead dog. "I have not sinned against you, yet you want to take my life?"

The foregoing really isn't rational. In the history of mankind, hell—the hell that is latent here among us, rampaging in the individuals on this diminutive globe, in our peers, even finding its way into us—is this senseless hatred, which has no need of sober justification; it does quite well without it.

Hatred felt before there is justification is the devil of history, a devil with extraordinary stamina, since it is nurtured by a suspicious imagination; this devil devours ideas, and munches with special pleasure on mixed metaphors.

355. David talks to the Lord. Before all his important decisions, he consults the Lord, who tells him something, gives him advice. They are on direct speaking terms, they need none of your prophet-interpreters. The reason we can say that David is chosen is that the Lord speaks with him. His is a loneliness shared with God, but it is dark in the depth of the cave, and the shadows of the night are frightening even to the slayer of lions.

The psalmist is happy, he has someone to turn to, but sometimes the persecuted one cannot sing, sometimes he just shivers and trembles and does not hear the fluttering wings of angels, only those of bats.

The biographer, whom we may call fate or the Lord's decision, must have the image of final abandonment: it is the only way that David's later reward can have the authority of fairy-tale justice. There are trials on the way to kingdom and the hand of the princess. The image of everyone's lining up in his favor is credible only if everyone abandons him first.

One may pity the young David in his great sadness, but it is consoling to know that he has not yet done anything to make him turn against himself. Consoling, but not especially dramatic. David becomes truly worthy of pity when he begins to mount up sins as king, either because he uses or doesn't use his power. His errors cause deaths. One cannot be king and not make mistakes. The Lord chose him, then strikes down on him in time.

356. If you are capable of contrition, or if the choice falls upon you, the angel will come to you, you will hear a voice, you will see a vision, and you will feel that the Lord is with you, that He is there where you are, because as you stand in the sand, you are visible from up high.

You must have a kind of conscience, an interior voice that can be soft or loud and is not removable by any kind of self-inflicted lobotomy.

Man carries God within himself, but he cannot identify with Him. He has pushed Him far enough away so that no kind of "hot" intimacy with Him is possible. But He is close enough so that man cannot hide from Him, not anywhere. This double hide-and-seek lasts forever—sometimes Adam hides from the Lord, sometimes the Lord is hidden from us, perhaps pulling the smoke of the crematorium in front of Himself as a veil.

357. Without the Lord above you, your arrogance would know no bounds. You need the man and the king—the Lord's Christ, in other words—above the one anointed by the prophet; you need the greater, infinite power. One requires the existence of a will higher than one's own, so believed the ancient Jews, who perceived how ephemeral idols are.

The Lord is a multiplication of the savage morals of the age, because He can become infinitely angry, and He is angry more often than elated. At times He punishes excessively, other times, when His hand is about to strike down, He orders it to stop, only He knows why. He is the God of the era's wild men. Every period, every people has an image of God that resembles it. The God of human beings also has a history, a growing-up story. He is beyond everything and infinitely far away, but to the inside of everything infinitely close.

We read that God sends His evil spirit upon the guilty. Therefore He has good and evil emissaries. The contradictions that human nature manifests are all in the biblical stories. That's why David, God's anointed one, is an appropriate literary figure in this great family novel. Through his deeds and words we learn something about the relationship between man and God. The one who speaks of God in the Psalms is a person whose actions we know.

358. Every little boy wants to be chief or king, and the great fairy tale is when it actually happens to one of them. To inherit the throne is less interesting, one only has to murder the brothers who covet it. David is the self-made king. The successful king, to boot. The boy with the slingshot who unifies the country, writes poetry, plays the lute, dances, makes love, and is a prophet too; every man will recognize in David something to which he aspires. Charlemagne wanted to be the new David, Michelangelo saw in him the perfect youth.

Solomon was wiser perhaps, but he wasn't the star, and biographers trace Jesus's family tree not back to him but back to the founding father who became king by his own strength, unified the southern and northern parts of the country, occupied Jerusalem and established it as the capital and the site of the Temple.

King David subordinated himself to the prophets, he did not become a God-king, but he didn't allow priestly rule either. David and Solomon were men of sensible compromise, spiritually directed Realpolitik; they obtained unity among the prophets and soldiers, among tribes and the apparatus of government. But all such balances are fragile by nature; this one broke up after Solomon.

359. The decadence that follows only makes the uniqueness of David's perfection more melancholy. His perfection is aesthetic rather than ethical, as that of a character in a novel. David is perfect, though for all those who died because of him, he was not

perfect. His truth is aesthetic, which requires a higher kind of understanding than purely ethical judgment, because aesthetic truth is richer and has more aspects; it considers the individual as a whole, though it doesn't disregard the rigorous antipodes of sin and sanctity.

There is no place on today's globe where David's story would be incomprehensible; today's adolescents would like it, and today's elderly could also recognize in it the model of manliness, of the man who knows there is a Lord above him. They would recognize the man of action, who decides according to God's advice, as he understands it, the man for whom loyalty, moral appropriateness, and inspired clear vision are the highest values. He is the man of action and prayer.

360. How can power be lawfully obtained and lawfully passed on according to the sensibility of the era? A parable of the lawful kingdom. The story makes it clear that the one who becomes king is the one anointed by the prophet, at God's prompting.

The prophet, or the Lord for whom he interprets, sometimes makes such wild demands that it is calming to know that he does not have kingly power. The prophet is quiet for a long time and appears occasionally as the seer of misfortune, or as the emissary of misfortune. And what is misfortune but a message from God?

Here is man's hopeless endeavor to interpret events as lessons of fate, as the warning of providence, as reward or punishment, so that he can see some kind of moral sense in fate.

But if God is responsible for events, He is unjust. Or? He is not responsible, because He does not exist. These two thoughts had to be driven from the consciousness of the Jews, because if they do not believe in the great ally, then they do not exist either. Then it is more practical to convert to one faith or another, at least for the sake of appearances. The hardly believable must be believed in spite of everything.

361. David dances the sacred dance before the Ark of the Covenant and before the Lord, accompanied by all Israel's cheers and music from the bugle, zither, lute, and drum. He takes home the dangerous ark, the one that kills those who touch it inopportunely. It should be near him but not in his house; let the priests guard it. They take the Ark of the Lord to its place by oxcart. Because there is only one ark, the ark is fragile.

There is one sacred ark, it cannot be reproduced, but what is inside—the voice put into words, those commands and prohibitions, the differentiation of right and wrong, the word, the story, and the poem—can be passed on. No matter whether King David wrote the psalms or whether they were written around him, these were the kinds of songs performed in his court, to the accompaniment of cypress-wood instruments, these were the songs people danced to, most likely drunk from wine and from addressing the Lord. They have been sung for three thousand years since, in various temples.

362. As close as David felt to the Lord is how high he jumped in his devout dance, while adoring women circled him. Mikal, the first wife, the daughter of King Saul, the cool princess, who did not bear a child despite having several husbands, saw David from the window. She was not pleased by the sight of David leaping about like a billy goat; he had climbed up to her side from the sheepfold, and she "despised him in her heart."

She will get her comeuppance: the Lord will make it known to her, through David, that she will not have children. Because David doesn't touch her anymore? Or perhaps he touches her, and she still doesn't conceive?

The king sees things differently than the wife. The people, the tribes, and the priesthood are all temporarily reconciled with one another; there is no great external threat. If the Lord appears to bless the united kingdom for the moment, then the founder of the capital city jumps up to the sky in joy and dances like a crazy man before the Lord; he would leave his own body if he could, and he embraces all.

The deal stands, let's drink, people! Tap the barrels! Pita and dates for everyone, the Covenant is validated. The prophet told David that his house and reign would endure forever.

363. Such a promise can be interpreted in many different ways. The story of David survives. Then the Lord elevates David's successor, who is of his blood and will build a house in praise of the Lord and make the kingdom stable (the kingdom of Solomon, the son of David and Bathseba). If David transgresses, "he is punished with the rod of men and with the stripes of the sons of men, but He does not remove His steadfast love."

As far as the rod and the stripes are concerned, the promise was kept. But what about the love? Not completely exterminated is the people that stubbornly tries to maintain a direct speaking relationship with God, avoiding all possible humanly imagined identifications of the Lord's image, since God is God exactly by being beyond what we can imagine. This need to think of the Almighty as beyond everything that can be depicted is a notion that cannot help but survive the millennia, no matter how turbulent they are.

The Lord cannot be seen with our eyes, but He can be heard as a voice in our souls. This peculiar combination of visual pessimism and auditory optimism could come only from authors, from the people of books.

David is confident that at least some of his successors will be anointed, chosen, pleasing to the Lord. Many will be worthy, but they will not all be chosen. Perhaps one of them will succeed in understanding David's legacy: The shepherd of a flock of sheep can be the shepherd of his people.

David, the smallest, became the greatest: he went through the experience of being down and then up, his story makes him lord over all of us, he is the best known image of ruler in Bible-reading countries. David is the parable of the ruler anointed and chosen by God. The prophet lets him know he will be king; this is the task David must accomplish meritoriously.

We read the tale of a king, a frail human, not an unbelievable saint, not a madman, not a sorcerer, not a miracle worker; he is not made grotesquely one-sided, he can swing to either pole of the pendulum. It is precisely his frailty that makes him our brother.

We share David's contempt for betrayal, and he is our brother in his meekness too. We have similar concepts of honor. He is close and yet far away, because among human fauna it is rare to find someone who has power and still can see himself as nothing.

364. In these ambivalent situations, David's elevated sense of loyalty leads him to unusual decisions, ones superior to the dictates of expediency. Every single life situation tests him with opposing promptings. He is the man of reality through and through, not a prophet, though he sometimes prophesies, just like Saul, whose place he takes.

He is many-sided. He listens to the prophet but is driven by a political goal: the unification of the northern and southern countries, Israel and Judah, the unification of the cults of Eli and Yahweh in tribally neutral, only recently occupied, but militarily and aesthetically advantageous Jerusalem, where he doesn't exterminate the local Jebusites according to the custom of the age but, rather, integrates them.

David is not just a military leader, he is an organizer of life and a creator of structure as well. He places both the royal palace and the Temple—home of the Ark of the Lord—in Jerusalem, near each other but nevertheless separate. He separates the state from the cult. He has a political vision, which he accomplishes with prophetic assistance. He avoids the criminal route to becoming king, thus he can be a mythologically approved, lawful king.

There is another aspect of David's story, which we could call the power of conscience. A transcendent demand of conscience, originating from God, conveyed by the prophet: this is the highest master. David lifts his conscience above himself, toward the Lord, he empowers the priests, he can transcend direct interests, he can turn against himself, he is capable of sin and guilt, he can win and he can lose. We see him at the head of the triumphal march—surrounded by adoring women—dancing his flamboyant dance, which his wife hates. He dances drunkenly, inebriated with himself, the cheers, and public acclaim.

365. Short is the thrill, long is the expiation.

If the king happens to walk on the roof of the palace instead of being with his troops in combat, perhaps it is because he has had enough of killing. If the king looks out the window, sees and desires a woman of considerable beauty as she bathes in the company of her friends and her servants, and if, at his request, his people bring him the woman, named Bathsheba, and if he lies with her and makes her pregnant, then he has fallen into the sin of excess, since he has his own wives and has inherited, moreover, the harem of his predecessor, Saul. There are quite enough women waiting for David. Still, up to now, no great sin has been committed.

David did not want this woman for only one night; he wanted her entirely, along with the child she would bear; he did not want to share her with her husband, Uriah, who was his loyal officer. Uriah was ordered to attack in battle, while his men were ordered to leave him alone at a certain moment, whereupon the enemy soldiers cut Uriah down. The order to deceive and betray Uriah was given by the king.

366. The Lord sends a message to David through the prophet Nathan: He has given David everything, and would have given him more, but it was not enough for David, he was insatiable,

therefore the Lord will take away what he has. Because David satisfied his desire through force of arms, arms will never leave David's house entirely, and trouble will also come from within his own house, from his concubines.

First, the Lord punishes David by letting the child of the marriage of force die. The king is able to suffer, to cry, to fast, and to beg for Bathsheba's infant not to die. He tries to make contact with the Lord, he repents, he would like to save the life of his son by Bathsheba, his favorite wife, the one acquired in sin, but the infant dies.

The King and Bathsheba had to live on, they still had to beget Solomon, the profound modernist, the outstanding cynic of the age. Solomon understood the distance from man to God, he understood that between the two the process of the world takes place, in which everything has its proper time.

By the time Bathsheba's second son becomes king, David's other sons have all killed one another, they defile their half sister, and they have their way with the wives of the enfeebled father-king, they dishonor the house of the king's concubines, they carry their vendettas to the death.

The royally exaggerated expansion of the patriarchal family leads to its collapse from within. Everything is taken away from the man who wants too much once he grows weak and old, once he is weighed down by guilt and doubt, once love without desire starts to predominate in him.

Who does the woman belong to? Who gets the woman? Believable stories of men. They are not saints but polygamists who follow the demands of their senses with less inhibition than the men of today, they steal wives for themselves. The sons pride themselves on bedding not their mothers but their father's other concubines. The rebellious son goes into his father's harem in plain sight of everyone. The vanquishing of the royal father, the son rising to his place, and the father resisting: this is the elemental story, which repeats itself among men just as it does in the herd.

David is a normal male, regularly visited by mercy and temptation, he is just and God-fearing, but at the same time he is a barbarian who has no trouble ordering that someone be killed. He has many wives, he is sensual and falls in love, he loves his women and is true to them. Mikal was once his wife; though she lives with someone else, he wants her to be his again, he takes her back so that she may live near him. He wants to enjoy having a large family, but it becomes a den of vipers.

Many sons from many concubines, at court they are unrestrained and envious, they offend one another, take revenge, and commit incest with a half sister, then are disgusted by the one they raped. Every scene has multiple meanings.

367. The fragments of a great novel are outlined here.

The merciless truth of great prose. There is no absolution. There is no black and white. Angel and sinner are in the same skin. There is the sin that a person wants and the sin that a person absolutely does not want but commits nonetheless.

Everyone goes along the road fate has ordered for them. The story has inner logic: David's son Absalom must rebel against his father. The father-king gullibly sends Absalom's little sister Tamar to Amnon, a son from another concubine. Amnon rapes her and then despises her. Absalom kills Amnon, and David cannot really forgive him, which explains the patricidal impulse. Every figure is credible, every act realistic.

David is not divine, though he is sometimes wise and can tell good from bad, like the angel of God. The Almighty chose him to be king, but being chosen is not the gateway to tranquillity, and even less a guide to happiness. The ones God chooses to rule are chosen for trouble, contrition, devotion, struggle, and suffering. And every act brings its due punishment. They kill a lot in

236 / The Invisible Voice

that world. David may have a little less of the passion to kill; he can restrain himself, he has a heart and can bow down before God.

368. "For my sake protect the young man Absalom!" With these words he sends his army into battle against Absalom, who has arbitrarily declared himself king and is preparing to kill his father so that the throne will be unquestionably his. "Spare only the boy!" asks the aged David. But if they do not spare Absolom's warriors, they won't spare Absalom either. A terrible death: he is caught, perhaps by his hair, on an oak tree, and Joab, the commander, the man loyal to the king, though aware of the king's will, thrusts three darts into the suspended body, and once it lies on the ground, he sets his bodyguards upon it, to stamp out any remnants of life.

"My son, Absalom! My son, my son, Absalom!" Thus moans the old king when his loyal army beats down the rebellious troops and kills the boy. As a rebel trying to seize the throne, Absalom got what he deserved, according to the customs of the time and according to what must have been the will of the army. Why should they bleed, if not for victory? Many of them die, let the chief of the enemy die too, so that victory will be complete. The army returns triumphantly and hopes for a joyous holiday, but the king cries and whimpers. Then the hardened general comes and reproaches the king—for loving those who hated him and because David probably would have regretted the death of those fighting for him less than the death of the boy. Let the king come out of the palace, finally, among the people and the soldiers.

David sits out in front of the city gate, distraught, and from then on he just shivers. He still has his wits, he is generous, or at least makes cautious decisions, but he is always cold. The council of elders make a most attentive decision; they order a virgin to his side, to warm him up at night. The reporters, who know even what goes on under the blankets, conscientiously add that although David did sleep with the virgin, he did not know her. David's story is all heartrending paradox. He preserved his life, his wives, the concubines, a court and military loyal to him, the dignity of the throne, but where is his son?

369. David is capable of stepping out of his role and empathizing with the other, even with his enemy. The capacity for empathy distinguishes him from those surrounding him.

The defeated one is killed. It is an elemental and barbarian world, this one in which a covenant is born between a people and a moral authority.

I don't know that I have to regard this text as the sacred word. I regard it as a novel. The great narratives are parables for every age.

David is the active type of protagonist. He initiates, builds, maintains, and defends. Those who act fall into sin. But not to act is impossible. He gives God His due, but he gives the job of being king its due as well, and it is not easy to do both.

In the book of Samuel, the prospects of hope resemble those of a corpse in a sarcophagus, but David gets out of it. Readers of the story again will recognize themselves in it, the things they desire and the things they cannot escape, because the careers even of the most glorious figures end in defeat. Something remains, however: Solomon, the son of the favorite wife, Bathsheba, the stolen one—and the foundation of the Temple.

The greatness of this Biblical narrative is that it doesn't allow all justice to reside in any one individual, it sees and admits the price of all actions and recognizes that life is all choices, choices that sometimes result in terrible loss. Still, there are better and worse decisions, decisions more and less pleasing to God, and even if you do what the angel advises, you can still commit a sin requiring penance, a sin from which no one can absolve you;

because it has been committed and cannot be undone, we live with it even when we enjoy ourselves. David's story does not authorize triumphant arrogance.

This novel or, let's say, chronicle would not have survived had it not been classified sacred. But only one thing is sacred in this story: human justice, the justice of the novel, the complicated justice of a kingdom existing in this world, in the midst of enemies.

370. One response to the military defeat of the kingdom—the physical defeat, the occupation by the empire—is disappearance, or assimilation. There is another possibility: spiritual ascendancy. But that also takes the form of kingdoms.

Another answer: to create the nation-state. People have been doing that diligently ever since; much gain and much evil are the consequences. The other possibility is to say that what belongs to the emperor is his, let him have it. But if even Constantine converts—if removing oneself from human conditions, families, and states becomes the national religion—certain difficulties spring up again.

Great statesmen are distinguished from great monsters by having made moral judgments and decisions that spared people, by having not always heeded the call of short-term interest but listened to the prompting of longer-term interests as well. The field of action was limited; much violent death clung to the decisions needed to establish the greatness of statesmen. David was great too, and many died because of his existence. The same thing has happened with every king who shaped some kind of lasting unity from his people.

371. A God wanted to exist, a God wanted a cult for himself. A God-hypothesis wanted devoted defenders, who—if they were men—were willing to comply or, more precisely, to make their infant sons comply with the requirement of circumcision, which

is healthy anyway. There emerges a picture of a priestly people that chooses itself for this special role. This people had to eschew the comfortable paths, the God-compromises made according to the many kinds of local interest. It signed on for exclusive monotheism: there is no other God. In the kingdom of David, a relatively stable, plural organism came into existence, one that maintained a complex negotiating relation between the spiritual and the material.

372. If there is a moral meaning to this story, it lies exactly in its justness, that it probably did happen that way, it had to happen about that way, it is credible. This is how a person faces his own situation when he hears divine voices. Perhaps there will be a battle tomorrow, perhaps he will no longer be alive tomorrow. Should he go or not? Should he take the challenge or not? The hero must decide constantly, and because he is chosen and anointed by a prophet, his actions will set an example. He asks for help to make the decisions, he requires the connection to God, he is entitled to that dialogue. He is entitled to have the Lord appear before him, to hear a voice or a call, to be visited by an angel.

Man's relation to power is illustrated through three kings. Saul battles for it; David creates it; Solomon steers it, makes it grand, and arrives at the recognition that it is all in vain, he can see the end. These three kings traverse the ballistic career arc of power. I have read few greater narratives about antiquity; their story is more modern than Homer, more Shakespearean. In this chronicle is the human condition, the continuous struggle with our dualities. On the one side is a divine voice that constantly demands something of us, on the other side is what we happen to be doing in the world, the here and now, our world, this world.

In the figure of the prophet, the poet is also a message-carrying master, a spiritual entity accepted and followed by many; he is occasionally tortured or even killed for being a prophet, but his vision of the nation's strategic orientation may sometimes be confirmed centuries later.

373. The greatest figure of the Old Testament is Moses, the stuttering chief who walked with God and brought us the greatest message, the Ten Commandments written on stone tablets, the moral fundament of the entire Judeo-Christian world, and the point of departure for other texts, like the Sermon on the Mount.

The priestly authors write and edit texts, they deliver chronicles, the fundamental tales we need. We long for tales of spring in the month of the bull, for images of spring, like the young David who arrived in Canaan, probably the greatest figure of post-Moses Jewry, if for no other reason than that most of the writing is devoted to him and most of the psalms are attributed to him. Because he is the most often sung poet, Christians and Jews use his words when they call God.

374. Religion is more than a call—it is action too. Moses and David do not just preach the word, they also implement it in the roles of prophet-chief and king. They challenge their environments with the prophetic mission, and they achieve it using the instruments of politics, including killing. In return, God denies them complete success. Moses does not enter the Promised Land. David, who creates the kingdom, conquers Jerusalem and makes it the capital, the spiritual and political capital, but if the founder-king can lay the foundation stone for the Temple, only Solomon can build it, because in the course of his lawfully inherited reign, Solomon happens to kill less than his father.

375. Of the worldly biblical figures, why did David become the central hero of the Bible? Because he is the freshest, the one we understand best, the one with whose decisions we can empathize.

The prophets cannot keep the tribes together; there is a need for kings that seem divine. With David began a new chapter in the ancient drama of spiritual and physical power, one that has run continuously throughout human history. An ideal king lives in the consciousness of Bible readers—he made the right decision in almost everything, but his passionate nature led him to sin. That's David.

1997

Ⓧ 49/7/14   #110315- JEWSH

14⁰⁰

8 ⁵⁰